THE DEVIL'S SHADOW
The Story of Witchcraft in Massachusetts

In 1692, in Salem Town, the extraordinary allega-
tions of a small group of hysterical girls brought
to trial five women. The charge against the accused:
witchcraft. The penalty: death. Thus began the in-
famous witchhunts of Massachusetts, and before
they ended, hundreds of innocent people had been
barbarously imprisoned or sent to the gallows. Behind this violent outbreak of persecution lay centuries of superstition. Nurturing it was a Puritan
culture so strict that it crushed all human feelings
and bred only fear and unrest. It was natural that
the girls should turn to Tituba for excitement. She
could tell fortunes, make love potions and exorcise
the devil. Meeting in secret, she so filled them with
wild tales of the "black art" that they felt bewitched
and called upon to exorcise the devil in others. The
charges brought against the hundreds of women
and men were senseless, and the trials themselves
travesties of justice. What was even more shocking
was the fact that so pitifully few voices were raised
in opposition. When the madness at last subsided,
it left in its wake a sense of shame that could never
be erased from the hearts of those who had taken
part in it. In this incredible story, full of terror and
drama, the author points up the truth of history itself being more strange than fiction.

Books by Clifford Lindsey Alderman

THE DEVIL'S SHADOW
   The Story of Witchcraft in Massachusetts

JOSEPH BRANT
   Chief of the Six Nations

LIBERTY, EQUALITY, FRATERNITY
   The Story of the French Revolution

THAT MEN SHALL BE FREE
   The Story of the Magna Carta

THE DEVIL'S SHADOW

The Story of Witchcraft in Massachusetts

by
Clifford Lindsey Alderman

Map and Drawings

JULIAN MESSNER
NEW YORK

Published simultaneously in the United States and Canada by
Julian Messner, a division of Simon & Schuster, Inc.,
1 West 39 Street, New York, N.Y. 10018. All rights reserved.

Fourth printing, 1968

Printed in the United States of America
Library of Congress Catalog Card No. AC 67-10629

Contents

Contents

THE DEVIL'S SHADOW
The Story of Witchcraft in Massachusetts

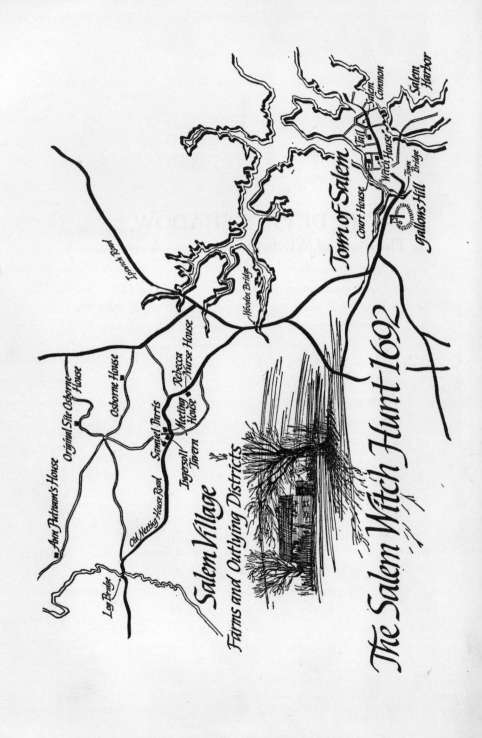

The Salem Witch Hunt 1692

Salem Village
Farms and Outlying Districts

Ann Putnam's House
Original Site Osborne House
Osborne House
Old Meeting House Road
Samuel Parris
Meeting House
Rebecca Nurse House
Ingersoll Tavern
Log Bridge
Ipswich Road
Wooten Bridge

Town of Salem
Court House
Witch House
Jail
Salem Common
Salem
Salem Harbor
Salem Hill
Town Bridge
Gallows Hill

1

The Execution

On the morning of July 19, 1692, a large farm cart drew up before the jail on Prison Lane in Salem Town. It was a small wooden building of one story, weather-beaten, unpainted and shabby. Inside, it was dim in spite of the sunshine of the summer day, for its barred windows were few and small. A stale, offensive stench filled the place, for the prisoners crowded into it had been there for many weeks without conveniences for keeping themselves clean.

Five women were confined in the darkness of the jail's stone-walled dungeon to prevent any possibility of their escape. Now, in the flickering light of a lantern, the jailer, William Dunton, moved among them, knocking the iron pins out of the shackles in the chains about the women's legs.

Most of them made no outcry, but one old woman moaned softly and shrank away as Dunton came toward her.

"Why do you come?" she muttered.

"It is time to go now, Goody Nurse." Dunton spoke in a loud voice, for she was very deaf.

"Lord, have mercy on me!" she cried.

Freed of their fetters, the five women were led out of the dungeon and delivered into the hands of the waiting sheriff of Essex County, George Corwin. Outside the jail a crowd was gathered, waiting. A sound arose among them as the prisoners appeared. It was not loud, but more like the distant rush of waters.

The five women might all have been sleepwalkers, for they seemed not to know where they were going or what was to happen to them. They had to be assisted as they tottered toward the cart. Then they were half pushed, half lifted up a plank placed to form a ramp up to the floor of the vehicle.

The cart drove off. It had difficulty in getting through narrow Prison Lane, for the throng there was vast. As it turned a corner, still more people lined the main street. They wore the austere dress of Puritans. The men were clad in somber coats and breeches and plain, wide-brimmed, high-crowned hats; the women's costumes too were dark, unadorned and relieved only by white caps, aprons, collars and cuffs.

Everyone in Salem Town was there, it seemed, as well as hundreds from the surrounding countryside for miles around. This was the second largest settlement in Massachusetts Bay and usually buzzed with activity. But today the shops where glaziers, chair makers, coopers, chandlers, weavers and shoemakers plied their trades were deserted. From the shipyards along the waterfront came no bedlam of hammers, mauls, saws and adzes. At the wharves, instead of the rattle of windlasses loading and unloading cargo, the only sound was the soft creak of mooring lines as the tall ships there stirred uneasily in the surge of the tide.

Some of the watching people reviled the five women: "Yah, witches!"

"Let your master the devil save ye now!"

"Repent, repent, ye wicked witches!"

"Witches, confess your sin!"

A few shook their fists. Others spoke words from Scripture:

"Ye shall be burned with fire and brimstone in hell!"

"It is the day of the Lord's vengeance!"

"The day of thy calamity is at hand, saith the Lord!"

For the most part, however, the people were silent. Their faces were stony. Yet shadows of uneasiness clouded their blank expressions when they looked at one another.

A woman spectator half whispered to her neighbor, "That's Susanna Martin of Amesbury—the plump one. How she's changed."

"Aye," said the other woman, "I saw her at the examination after they arrested her. Pretty, she was, and neat in her dress. Look at her now—she's aged twenty years . . . and those rags she's wearing . . . and *dirty!* Guess she's sorry now . . ."

The first woman sniffed. "She's got no one but herself to blame—making a contract with the devil. Flew to Newbury on a broomstick in the muddy season to see her friend, didn't she? Her friend *knew* . . . wasn't a trace of mud on her shoes. How'd she get there but through the air?"

But to herself the woman thought: *Is Susanna Martin really a witch? Suppose ... suppose her friend in Newbury who cried out on her had a grudge ...*

She flashed a sidelong glance at her companion. *What's she thinking? That argument we had last week ... I had the best of her, but is she waiting to get even? What can I do if she cries out on me?*

A man among the spectators thought: *Who will be next? No one is safe. My neighbor Wilkins ... he's been grumpy since I bought the piece of land that makes my farm bigger than his. Is he jealous? Would he like to see me* in that cart?

Behind the pitiless stares on the faces in the crowd there was fear ...

As for the wretched creatures in the cart, they saw or heard little of all this. Their minds were numb with terror and despair. They clung weakly to the sides of the cart to keep from falling, not only because of its jolting but from faintness.

The multitude lining the street closed in to follow the cart as it lurched westward. It reached the outskirts of the town, where the dwellings thinned out and there were only occasional farmhouses in the midst of fields and meadows.

Ahead loomed a rocky ridge. It stood out starkly against the sky, for its highest point was mostly bare ledge, save for a few ancient trees. The cart drove on toward the northern end of the ridge. Then it turned off into a rough, rutted road that was little more than a path rising toward the summit. Going up, the horses strained at the load while the driver cursed and lashed at them with his whip. And at last the cart reached the desolate crest of Gallows Hill.

Below it spread a vast expanse of sea, harbor, field and woodland. To the east sprawled Salem Town, its close-packed houses jostling each other about the barnlike meetinghouse. Beyond, white sails dotted the harbor, and the bare masts and spars of the ships at the wharves were like trees swept by a forest fire. To the south, west and north, a great hilly wilderness stretched into the distance. Here and there it was broken by cleared farm-lands and their dwellings, the houses of a village, the gleam of a pond or stream.

Behind the cart the people scrambled to the summit, spreading themselves out over it like a black cloak thrown down upon its rocks and boulders. They had no eyes for the panorama below them. Their gaze was fixed upon a dreadful sight.

From the lower branches of the gnarled trees that clung to the sparse soil of the summit hung five stout ropes, each with a noose at its lower end. Resting against one of these branches was a ladder.

The cart had stopped now, backed up to the ladder. The silence on Gallows Hill was ghastly. As they waited, the spectators held their breaths. It was as if each of them were there in place of the woman the sheriff was pushing and lifting out of the cart and onto the ladder.

Each might have been feeling the roughness of the rope's strands as it was dropped over the condemned woman's head, the trembling terror of the instant before the ladder was whisked away, the sickening drop, the convulsive jerk, the desperate struggle for breath . . .

Some gazed as if their eyes were riveted to the sight by an unseen force which would not let them look away. Some did turn away in horror. Four times the ladder was shifted to a new position while the cart backed up to it, four more times came the terrible dance of death.

Once, as one of the five mounted the ladder, a voice came without warning, chilling the people's blood:

"Sarah Good, you are a witch, and you know you are a witch!"

It was a minister, the Reverend Nicholas Noyes of the First Church of Salem Town.

Indeed, Sarah Good resembled what the people thought a witch should look like, with her weather-beaten face, her hair in matted disorder, her eyes wild and staring.

"You are a liar!" she flung at Mr. Noyes just before the ladder was snatched from under her. "I am no more a witch than you are a wizard, and if you take my life, God will give you blood to drink!"

A shudder passed through the spectators.

It was over at last. The crowd dispersed down the slope of Gallows Hill. They did not look at each other now, for each feared to see in another's face what was in his own thoughts. In fascination, some ventured a quick glance back at the hilltop where the five motionless figures dangled, silhouetted against the sky. None could shut out the thud of spades behind them, or the clang when one struck a rock, for the graves were being dug in a shallow crevice between the ledges.

Sarah Good, Sarah Wildes, Elizabeth Howe, Susanna Martin and Rebecca Nurse, all convicted of practicing witchcraft, had been executed according to the stern vengeance of Puritan law in Massachusetts Bay. They were early victims of the witchcraft delusion which swept the colony in the year 1692.

As they went away, the people tried to tell themselves: They had to die. It is in the Bible—"Thou shalt not suffer a witch to live." They *were* witches. They tortured those poor children in Salem Village—pinched and bit and beat them. They had sold their souls to Satan. It was all proved in court.

Yet doubt nagged insistently at them, though each would have denied it: What if they *weren't* witches?

Nonsense, they insisted to themselves. Everyone knows there are witches. There are many more of them in Massachusetts Bay. They must be hunted down and destroyed, every last one of them.

Why, then, did they go silently to their houses, avoiding each other? Was it because, in their hearts, there was guilt . . . ?

2

The Black Art of Witchcraft

The people of Massachusetts Bay were by no means the first to believe in witchcraft. The origins of the belief go so far back into bygone centuries that they are lost in the mists of antiquity.

Certainly the ancient Hebrews knew of witchcraft, for witches, sorcerers and wizards are often mentioned in the Old Testament of the Bible. So did the people of other nations of that time, some three thousand years ago. In fact, no nation in history, whether savage or civilized, has been entirely free of beliefs in witchcraft.

Persecution and punishment of people thought to be witches or wizards (male witches, also called warlocks) did not become widespread in Europe until the fifteenth century. At that time the Church of Rome decided that sorcery was a dangerous evil and must be exterminated. During the late fifteenth and early sixteenth centuries, thousands of persons were condemned as witches and executed in Italy and Germany.

In France, the most famous of the early "witches" was executed in 1431. Joan of Arc, a humble little shepherdess, loved her country intensely. England had invaded and occupied most of it, and the French king, Charles VII, had been deprived of his throne by Henry V of England. Joan had a vision in which she heard voices commanding her to drive the English out of France.

She placed herself at the head of ten thousand soldiers, defeated the invaders occupying Orléans and restored Charles VII to his throne. But she failed to liberate all of France, and at last she was taken prisoner. She was charged with being a witch, condemned and burned alive at Rouen. Today, far from being thought of as a witch, she is Saint Joan of Arc, and the anniversary of her death is celebrated as a holiday in France.

In England, persecution of accused witches did not become widespread until the latter part of the sixteenth century. The man chiefly responsible for it was King James I. Strangely, he is best known for a good work. He set scholars to producing a new and improved translation of the Bible, the famous King James Version, which is still in extensive use today.

If he had been satisfied to let scholars do his writing for him, he might have saved many of his people untold misery and suffering. But he wrote a book himself that loosed a veritable hornets' nest of persecution upon England and Scotland.

King James was coarse; his manners were often piggish, but he had a sharp, shrewd mind and took an interest in many things. One of them was witchcraft.

Probably he first turned his attention to it in Scotland. He ruled there as King James VI until Queen Elizabeth of England died, and he inherited her throne. The Scots were very superstitious, and their church, or Kirk, was the unrelenting enemy of witchcraft.

James investigated it thoroughly. Oddly, in the Bibles before the King James Version there were few references to witchcraft as such. Some scholars believe that James's translators, knowing his concern with the subject, included passages about it which may actually have had a slightly different meaning in the old Hebrew biblical manuscripts.

Now that he knew so much about witchcraft, King James wrote his book. Its title was *Demonology*. It had a profound influence in starting the wave of witchcraft persecutions that flooded over England and Scotland.

In his book the King stated his firm belief in some of the "tests" used to detect witchcraft, especially the one known as "swimming" an accused witch. This was done by throwing her into a pond or river. If she was really a witch the water would have none of her and she would float. Then she could be hauled out and executed. Of course, if she sank and drowned, her family and friends would have the satisfaction of knowing she died an innocent woman.

The book contained other examples of King James's belief in witchcraft. A Puritan named Matthew Hopkins read it. He was not only fascinated by the book but inspired to lead a campaign to exterminate every witch in England.

By that time it was near the middle of the seventeenth century. King James was dead and his son Charles I was on the throne. The Puritans had become powerful; soon they would behead King Charles, and their leader, Oliver Cromwell, would rule England as Protector. Their ministers were as unyielding enemies of witchcraft as were those of the Kirk in Scotland. It was the very time for a witch hunt.

Matthew Hopkins became known as the Witch-Finder-General. All over England he hunted down his prey. Some towns, hearing of his success, invited him to come and search out the witches who were doing all kinds of mischief in their midst. In two years Matthew Hopkins pointed out two hundred persons as witches; they were sent to the gallows.

In some European countries, more horrible methods of execution than hanging were used, especially the practice of burning condemned witches alive. Frightful tortures were applied too in order to force confessions from the wretched people accused of witchcraft. There were thumbscrews which could be tightened until a person suffered excruciating agony, instruments for gouging out the eyes, red-hot branding irons, and a fiendish device called The Question which could break every bone in one's body.

In England, however, such methods were not used during the late-seventeenth-century witchcraft persecutions. Accused witches were tried in court and then hanged if they were convicted. In fact, by that time many judges and some of the clergy were beginning to have some doubts about witchcraft.

Not the common people, however. Few had enough education to think clearly and reasonably. For centuries these superstitious people had believed in witches, wizards, sorcerers and other supernatural spirits. Stories of strange happenings, which they were sure could have been caused only by the devil and his creatures had been handed down in English families ever since the Dark Ages.

It was natural, when the settlement of America began in the early years of the seventeenth century, that the colonists should bring these beliefs with them. This was especially true of the Massachusetts Bay settlers, who were largely Puritans. Puritan belief in witchcraft was so strong that even learned men were convinced—doctors, schoolmasters, judges, officials of the government and particularly the ministers.

The very few who did not believe or who had doubts were usually careful to say nothing of their ideas. Otherwise they themselves might be suspected and their very lives would be in danger.

Almost everyone did believe, however. A farmer in one of the settlements would come in from the barn in the morning and say to his wife, "There's a witch about. The horse's mane is tangled where she knotted it for a stirrup to mount and ride off to a witches' Sabbath."

A witches' Sabbath, as everyone knew, was a gathering at which they practiced their secret rites and communicated with their master, the devil. Some stole horses to get there; others rode through the air on broomsticks.

The farmer's wife would nod wisely. "Thought 'twas funny the butter wouldn't come when I churned yesterday. I'll put a shilling into the churn the next time. That'll keep the witch away."

Or a Massachusetts Bay goodwife, putting a batch of bread to bake in the oven, would feel a little breeze as she opened the door. That was a witch gliding in to make the loaves fall flat or burn.

If a farmer's cow gave no milk, that was a witch's doing. The remedy was to tie a red tag to bossy's tail so the witch would not dare to sail into the barn and milk her dry. A witch could also dry up wells, make horses go lame, cause milk to sour and stir up a storm to destroy crops.

The story of what happened in Massachusetts Bay in 1692 really began a few years earlier, far to the south on the West Indian island of Barbados. Great fields of sugar cane were planted by the island's English settlers, for its soil and climate were perfectly suited to growing that profitable commodity. Large numbers of hands able to work under the hot tropical sun were needed to till the soil and tend and harvest the crop. Thus the curse of slavery fell upon Barbados when traders brought in shiploads of Negroes from the hot coast of Africa and sold them to the planters.

The sugar and molasses produced from the cane were in great demand in the American colonies, especially New England. Not only were they used for food, but distillers there turned them into even more profitable rum.

One of the merchants who lived in Boston and traded with Barbados was Samuel Parris. He had gone to Harvard College, intending to become a minister, but had changed his mind and left before graduating.

From Barbados, Mr. Parris obtained two slaves. Usually one thinks of slavery in America as belonging to the South, but although thousands of slaves were used in the tobacco and rice fields of the southern colonies, a good many northern settlers kept them too in colonial times.

It is not known whether Mr. Parris was actually living in Barbados when he bought the two slaves. He may have made voyages there in connection with his business, or his purchase of a woman and her husband may have been entrusted to the captain of one of his ships.

The woman, named Tituba, had been born in Barbados. One of her parents was a Negro, the other a Carib Indian. Her husband was a Carib. The records do not show his real name, but in Massachusetts Bay he became known as John Indian. Many of these natives of the West Indies, or Sugar Islands as they were often called, had been enslaved along with the African Negroes.

Tituba was happy in Barbados. She did not particularly mind being a slave, for she had never known freedom and thus did not miss it. She was lazy, and life on the island was easy. No one worked too hard in that warm climate. The sun shone brightly and there was plenty to eat.

Tituba knew a good deal about sorcery and the black art. Barbados was no more free of what was thought to be witchcraft than Europe was. In the West Indies it was known as obeah. All the black people believed in it.

Obeah was a kind of sorcery. Its leaders were witch doctors known as obeah men. They had great power over the other slaves and were very much feared.

The obeah man presided at secret rites in which weird dances were performed and goats or fowl sacrificed to the gods of the cult. On some of the islands children were stolen and sacrificed.

The obeah men claimed many magic powers. For those who paid them for their services, they predicted the future and drove away evil spirits. They prepared charms and love potions. They promised prosperity in business, success in love, protection against the "evil eye," and even caused a person's enemy to die.

Tituba and John Indian became servants in Mr. Parris's household. It was a great change for both slaves. Real winter was unknown in Barbados. Now they shivered in the icy blasts and blizzards of New England. They missed the warm sun that shone almost constantly on Barbados and dreaded the long dark days.

Nevertheless, in time they got used to it. Tituba was very fond of the Parrises' little daughter Betty. She gave the child tender care and kept her amused. And while life in Boston was not like the lazy days she had known in Barbados, she managed to satisfy Mr. and Mrs. Parris without working too hard.

Mr. Parris was learning that he had made a mistake in choosing a merchant's career. His business was not prospering. In 1689 he decided to give it up and enter the ministry after all.

None of the big churches in Boston wanted a minister who had not completed his theological studies. But to the north the little hamlet of Salem Village needed one. Its people could not afford a regular minister, and Mr. Parris was accepted. He would have to take part of his salary in corn and other things produced on the farms of his congregation, but a comfortable house would be furnished him rent free, and pasture land for cows and other livestock. With his family and the two slaves, he came to Salem Village.

It was there, in Mr. Parris's parsonage on a winter afternoon in 1692, that the stage was set for the terrible witchcraft delusion.

3
Tituba

Seated on one of the high-backed settles that faced each other across the chimney corner, Ann strained her eyes to catch the firelight's flicker on the piece of linen in her lap. Once, twice, three times her needle gave out a tiny flash as her deft fingers plied it swiftly back and forth. Then she leaned forward, seized the thread between her teeth and bit it off. She raised her head and held her work at arm's length. That line was done, thank goodness.

The characters, formed by thread dyed crimson in pokeberry juice, straggled across the sampler:

Ann Putnam   Aged 12   1692

Above them in yellow, was a verse:

When I was young and in my Prime,
You see how well I spent my time.
And by my sampler you may see
What care my Parents took of me.

Ann sighed. There was still the border to be embroidered, hundreds of tiny stitches to be taken, forming the intricate pattern. She hated doing samplers. Some of her prissy friends were perfectly content to sit hour after hour, sewing, sewing . . .

Ann's thoughts were gloomy ones. She was thinking of how dull life was in Salem Village, especially on a day like this one.

Outside the kitchen window, in the white world of midwinter, a dreary prospect of snowy fields undulated into the distance under skies that were the color of her mother's pewter, holding a promise of more snow. Against the whiteness of the meadows, the trees stood out starkly like skeletons thrusting up bony arms and fingers in gestures of despair. Bleak too were the farmhouses Ann could see, as alike as one day to another in this season. Their roofs were steep-pitched in front and long-sloping in the rear, their windows a latticework of diamond-shaped panes, chimneys squat and massive, each with its curling blue spiral of wood smoke.

Winter—ugh! It was an unending round of indoor drudgery—bedmaking, dusting, sewing, knitting, working samplers, combing wool, winding skeins, weaving. And spinning, always spinning—Ann had learned to spin on the great wheel when she was so small she had to stand on a footstool.

The only thing that broke the monotony in the winter was going to meeting on the Sabbath, and that was worse. Meeting was sitting on a hard, cold bench on the women's side of the broad aisle in the bare, unheated meetinghouse. It was suffering all through the morning and then the afternoon while Mr. Parris prayed forever and preached even longer. It was watching the hourglass on the pulpit, sure it must be clogged, for it seemed that the sand would never run down. It was trying to warm tingling toes on a footwarmer which had surely gone out, and feeling the savage cold creep into the very marrow of one's bones as it turned noses blue and fingers numb.

Ann Putnam couldn't imagine what got into her sometimes these days. Often she itched to do something that would shock people. More than once, in meeting, she had been seized with an overpowering urge to let out one good screech right in the middle of one of Mr. Parris's interminable sermons. It seemed to her it would be worth getting a sharp rap from the knobbed end of the tithingman's rod.

If only *something* would happen . . .

Ann's gaze shifted toward the inside of the room. It was lighted only by the dancing tongues of flame as they licked up into the vast throat of the fireplace, carrying the swirling sparks. The fire shed a soft radiance on the heavy, rough-hewn beams of the ceiling and lent something of its glow to the pewter ware in the corner cupboard and the smooth-worn surface of the trestle table in the center of the room. Above the clutter of pots, pans, gridiron, tongs and shovel on the hearth, the hasty pudding for supper bubbled and plopped in the great iron kettle which hung over the fire.

There was a sound like a clock's tick as Ann's mother, a vague shape on the opposite side of the kitchen, finished winding a knot of flax thread on the clock-reel. A line of a song flashed into Ann's mind. She had heard Mercy Lewis, the maidservant, singing it to herself one day, about a busy young woman and her suitor:

And he kissed Mistress Polly
When the clock-reel ticked.

Like Mistress Polly, Goodwife Putnam had stopped to tie the knot as the reel ticked to show that forty threads had been wound. In the dimness of the room, Ann saw her mother put her hand to her forehead.

"What is it, Mother?"

"It is nothing, child. Just one of my megrims."

"If your head aches, why don't you stop and lie down?"

"The work does not do itself, Ann. Forty threads to a knot, twenty knots to a skein, and stopping to rest won't change it. I've finished but one skein today." Her hand was still on her forehead. "I slept ill last night and there was the dream . . ."

"The dream, mother? The same . . . ?"

"Aye, the same. Your Aunt Bayley and her children and mine—the little ones who died before you were born—standing there in their winding sheets, stretching out their hands to me. It was just like all the other times —they were trying to tell me something, trying so hard, and I couldn't tell what it was they—"

She stopped short and gave her daughter a look that cautioned silence as Mercy Lewis came into the room. The maidservant was a slatternly wench of nineteen, sly-eyed, with untidy yellow hair.

"Have you finished in the parlor?" Goodwife Putnam asked her.

"Yes'm."

"Then there's an errand in the village. Mrs. Parris is poorly, they say, with a humor of the chest. Put some of my currant jelly in a porringer and take it to her, Mercy. Mayhap 'twill do her good, poor thing, though her affliction's more of the soul than body, I fear."

"Mother, may I go too?" Ordinarily Ann would not have asked on such a day. It was two miles to the minister's house, a cold journey afoot over a road that would be drifted in places. But today it seemed to her that she would go daft if she didn't get out somewhere, anywhere.

Goodwife Putnam looked disapproving. "There's your sampler—surely you've not finished it?"

Ann pouted. "No-o, but there's only the border . . ."

Goodwife Putnam's look plainly said "No," but suddenly her expression changed.

"Go, child, if you wish," she said.

Ann's spirits took wing. She and Mercy drew on their cloaks of decent gray homespun, stepped into the clogs that were like platforms built up on iron rings for walking in snow or mud, and started for the parsonage. Outside, as the sharp air took its pincers grip on their faces, they drew their hoods over the white-winged caps the Puritan women of Salem Village wore.

"Ann!" It was Goodwife Putnam calling from the doorway. "Come here a moment."

Ann went back to the door. Her mother drew her inside, out of reach of Mercy's sharp ears. "Child, if you see your chance, mayhap you can find out . . . about the dream . . ."

"But mother, won't Mr. Parris think such a thing sinful?"

A look of alarm crossed Goodwife Putnam's face. "No, child, not Mr. Parris! Tituba . . ."

"Tituba!" Ann stared.

" 'Tis said the natives of the Sugar Islands know ways of reaching the dead," Goodwife Putnam went on. Then her fingers closed on Ann's shoulder. "Say naught to the minister or Mrs. Parris about this! Mind, don't speak to Tituba if they are about!"

Puzzled, Ann rejoined Mercy Lewis and the two set out on the long trudge to the village center. Their drab figures, as they receded into the distance, looked almost like two crows, one small, one full-grown, stalking along.

"What did your mother want?" the maidservant demanded.

Mindful of Goodwife Putnam's warning, Ann gave the girl no satisfaction. "Nothing," she replied.

"Was it about the dream?" Mercy persisted.

"Dream? What dream do you mean, Mercy?"

"Don't get up on any high horses with me, mistress," said the girl tartly. "You know what I mean. She was talking about it when I came into the kitchen. The dream about her sister Bayley and the children. I've heard her tell of it before."

Mercy *had* been snooping, then. "Mother's not well," Ann said. "Something's on her mind."

"What's on her mind?"

"Things . . ."

Ann didn't want to say more, though she knew well enough what it was. Her mother had been Ann Carr, whose older sister Mary had married the Reverend James Bayley. When he became the minister in Salem Village and the couple moved there, Mary had brought her sister along. That was how Ann's mother had come to marry Sergeant Thomas Putnam of Salem Village.

There had been trouble from the start for Mr. Bayley, the same kind of trouble the next minister, Mr. Burroughs, had had. Some of the people in Salem Village hadn't liked Mr. Bayley. They spied on him, said Ann's mother, and hounded him too, until he had finally left, just as his successor, Mr. Burroughs, had. It was the way the people had persecuted the Bayley family, Goodwife Putnam had told Ann, that had caused first Mrs. Bayley's children and then Mrs. Bayley herself to die.

Mercy Lewis wasn't ready to give up. She echoed Ann's reply: "What things on her mind?"

"My mother . . . isn't well," Ann said slowly.

She herself wasn't too well, either, though nothing like her mother, who was pale and thin, with lines on her face; sometimes she flew into a rage over little things. Something was certainly amiss with her, Ann thought.

"I know she's poorly," Mercy replied, "but what's wrong with her?"

"I . . . don't know."

Mercy said nothing more for a few moments and they trudged silently over the snowy road, its ruts packed hard by passing farmers' sleds. They reached Beaver Dam Brook, about halfway to the village center, and crossed the little bridge there.

Then Mercy Lewis said, "Did you ever think . . . a witch might be doing it to her?"

Ann gasped. "Witches . . . in Salem Village?"

"Of course," said Mercy. "There's witches all over Massachusetts Bay. Why, 'twas scarce three years ago they hanged Goody Glover in Boston for bewitching those children."

Ann remembered. She had heard her father and mother talking about it at the time. And of course she knew there were witches everywhere. But in Salem Village it was mostly trifling mischief they were up to.

Of course the Bible proved that there were witches. Ann knew her Bible well. She was intelligent and had a quick mind which absorbed learning easily. There were very few books in Salem Village, but there was always the Bible.

Goodwife Putnam and Ann had already read it through together. Ann could quote from Exodus: "Thou shalt not suffer a witch to live"; from Leviticus: "A man also or a woman that hath a familiar spirit, or that is a wizard, shall surely be put to death"; and the longer one from Deuteronomy, which says that witches and other evil spirits are an abomination unto the Lord.

Yet when Mercy Lewis suggested that a witch might be at the bottom of Goodwife Putnam's troubles, Ann was stunned. If the servant girl were right it could mean that someone in Salem Village itself was putting a spell on her mother.

"But—but who'd want to do my mother harm?" she stammered.

Mercy tossed her head. "Who knows? There's plenty of queer ones in this village. Like old Goody Osburne or—or *her*."

The maidservant's elbow jabbed sharply into Ann's ribs and she looked up. Coming toward the girls was a crone whose greasy, uncombed gray locks streamed down over her shoulders. The voluminous skirts of her gown, billowing as she hobbled along, were stained and threadbare. As Sarah Good neared the girls she glared at them from rheumy eyes set in a seamed and leathery face, and muttered something Ann could not catch. And as she passed, the younger girl caught the choking reek of the stubby pipe the woman held clenched between blackened stubs of teeth.

Ann had heard all about Goody Good from her mother. No bit of gossip or scandal escaped Goodwife Putnam's ears. Sarah Good had no home. Her husband William "worked 'round" wherever help was needed. His wife and their clutch of children went with him, bedding down in haymows if there was no room in the house. When there was no work, Sarah begged from farm to farm.

A good many of the people in Salem Village wouldn't have her around. They didn't like her sharp tongue, for one thing. She scolded anyone who refused to give her alms or cast-off clothing. Some believed she had carried the smallpox when an epidemic of the dread disease had swept the village a few years before. And there was always the chance that she would set house or barn afire with her villainous pipe.

Ann could not repress a shudder. Goody Good *did* look like a witch . . .

At the village crossroads the girls turned to the right, passing Deacon Ingersoll's big house and tavern. The parsonage was only a short distance beyond, a larger house than most in Salem Village, with four big chimneys. They crossed the dooryard and Mercy raised and let fall the heavy knocker on the door.

For some moments there was no answer. Mercy was about to knock again when the door was swung open by the minister's daughter. Betty Parris was nine years old, with fair hair and blue eyes. She looked a little startled, like a child caught red-handed in some mischief.

"Oh, hello, Betty," said Mercy. "Goodwife Putnam sent us to ask after your mother and fetch her some jelly."

" 'Twas real good of her," Betty said, accepting the gift. "Dr. Griggs says Mother's some better today, but he bade her keep to her bed." She hesitated a moment. "Won't you—won't you come in?"

Ann said politely, "Pray, don't disturb your mother. We'll stay only long enough to warm ourselves before starting back. Is—is Mr. Parris about?"

"No," Betty replied, "he's over to Ingersoll's for a meeting of the parish committee."

"Where's Abigail?" Mercy asked. Ann noticed the little girl's guilty start at the question.

"She—we—we're . . . up with Tituba," Betty stammered.

Mercy Lewis pricked up her ears. "What are you doing up there, Betty?"

The minister's daughter glanced over her shoulder toward the staircase leading to her mother's bedchamber above. Then she lowered her voice. "Tituba's . . . telling our fortunes."

"La, what fun!" Mercy cried. "Take us up there, do, Betty."

"You—you won't tell?" the child asked.

"Of course not," said Mercy. "Come on, Ann."

Ann's mouth had fallen open. Fortunes . . . it was sinful . . . and right in the minister's house! She knew it would be wrong to go, but the reckless spirit that possessed her was prodding. Besides, there was her mother's message for Tituba. "All right," she said.

Betty Parris led the way back to the kitchen under the long rear slope of the roof, then up the narrow, breakneck stairs that rose to the garret above.

There, in a tiny, low-ceilinged bedchamber, Betty Parris's cousin Abigail Williams was seated on one side of the bed, Tituba on the other. Again Ann's mouth sagged in a gasp as she saw what was spread out on the coverlet between them. Playing cards—the devil's picture books!

Looking up as the three girls came in, Tituba flashed a wide grin that displayed teeth very white in comparison to the dark copper color of her skin. Yet for all her amiable expression there was something wild and strange in the gaze of the jet black eyes below her disorderly mop of straight black hair. But her voice when she greeted Ann and Mercy had a pleasant, lazy softness.

Abigail Williams was eleven. Ann had never liked her. She could be spiteful, and she had a look as though she knew things she was not telling. She was an orphan who had been adopted by Mr. and Mrs. Parris, her uncle and aunt.

No one knows just what happened on that bitter January afternoon up in Tituba's chamber. The slave probably told all the girls' fortunes, and no doubt the cards predicted for each such a fascinating future that they were charmed and delighted. It would have been all the more exciting because of the risk of getting caught at something which was strictly forbidden in Salem Village. Nor does anyone know what else they may have learned from Tituba.

That day in January was not the first or the last of such meetings in the parsonage. Tituba had already imparted some of her evil knowledge to Betty Parris and Abigail Williams, along with three older neighbor girls —Mary Walcott and Elizabeth Booth, who were sixteen, and eighteen-year-old Susanna Sheldon. Soon others joined the circle—three servant girls, Elizabeth Hubbard, Sarah Churchill and Mary Warren.

It was easy to find an excuse for visiting the parsonage. One might go to consult with the minister upon a spiritual matter needing guidance and prayer, perhaps to seek his explanation of a passage in the Bible or the catechism in which all children were instructed as required by law. In one way or another the girls managed to meet frequently with Tituba. Since they were careful, their elders, including Mr. and Mrs. Parris, suspected nothing.

Through Ann, Tituba must have given Goodwife
Putnam some reason to hope that she could get in touch
with her dead sister and the little ones. She encouraged
Ann to continue her visits to the parsonage.

At last, however, the meetings came to an abrupt end.
Betty Parris was sick. Then people heard that something
was wrong with Abigail Williams too. For a time that
was all anybody knew, for Mr. and Mrs. Parris said no
more than that. Even Goodwife Putnam's sensitive nose
was unable to smell out just what was going on.

But it is hard to keep a secret in a parsonage where
people constantly seek out the minister with their troubles. At last the stunned inhabitants of Salem Village
learned what had happened to Betty Parris and Abigail
Williams.

What had happened then spread to other girls in the
village faster than an epidemic of smallpox. First Mary
Walcott and Susanna Sheldon got it. Then one day
Goodwife Putnam saw that something was wrong with
her daughter.

Ann began to make strange sounds. First she muttered
to herself, then barked like a dog, then brayed like a
donkey. Before her mother's horrified eyes she got down
on all fours and began to scramble about under tables
and chairs, still making the animal-like sounds. Suddenly
she went into convulsions. She lay writhing on the floor,
uttering such terrible screams that it brought her father
on the run from the barn.

For a moment or two Ann's parents watched in a
panic, sure she was dying. Then Sergeant Putnam dashed
back to the barn, saddled a horse and rode headlong out

the Ipswich road to summon Dr. Griggs. By that time Mercy Lewis had collapsed beside Ann on the floor, adding her screams and writhings to the pandemonium.

This was the same thing that had already happened to Betty Parris, Abigail Williams, Mary Walcott and Susanna Sheldon. This was the beginning of the witchcraft delusion in Salem Village.

4

Mr. Parris Investigates

Dr. Griggs was the only physician in Salem Village, and he had already been called in to examine Betty Parris, Abigail Williams and the two neighbor girls. When he came to Sergeant Thomas Putnam's he did the same as he had with the others. He inspected the two girls' tongues, thumped on their chests with his knuckles and bent to listen to their hearts, asked questions, dosed them with medicines compounded of herbs and simples, pored through his medical books which had come from England. At last he shook his head in bewilderment and said, "The evil hand is on them."

Soon he had trouble in his own house, for Elizabeth Hubbard, who was his niece and also the family maidservant, came down with the mysterious malady. In fact, every one of the girls who had met at the parsonage became afflicted. People gathered to watch their strange antics and the fits in which they sometimes had to be held down to keep them from throwing themselves into the fire. The visitors shook their heads, half in pity, half in dread of whatever was causing this scourge that had fallen upon Salem Village.

Almost everyone felt great sympathy for the "afflicted children," as they were called, although several were almost grown up. There were a few hard-hearted souls in Salem Village, however, who declared the whole thing was a lot of fiddle-faddle. They suggested that a good hiding would put a stop to it sooner than Dr. Griggs' remedies. The other inhabitants were outraged at such a cruel attitude.

At first the people thought the best thing would be to let the epidemic run its course. They were encouraged when the girls came out of their fits and were perfectly normal once more. But no sooner was there an improvement than a new wave of twitchings, spasms and queer actions would sweep the village.

February was almost over when Mr. Parris decided that something drastic must be done. He wrote letters to the ministers of the surrounding villages, asking them to come for a consultation. A midwinter thaw had set in, but even roads that were quagmires could not keep the pastors away. Agog to see something of this mysterious visitation for themselves, they saddled their horses and floundered through the mud to Salem Village. The next morning, in the meetinghouse, the girls were brought before them.

Ann Putnam was there. As the ministers, one after another, rose to pray that the "children" might be restored to health, she and the other girls sat as if they heard nothing. But at last some began to shriek whenever the name of God or a sacred thing was mentioned. Then Ann was seized with a fit. As for Abigail Williams, her screams were so loud that the meetinghouse became a bedlam and the ministers had to give up.

When they saw that their attempt to pray the girls back to health had failed, it became plain that some dark and powerful force was opposing them. They must find out who or what was making the afflicted ones behave so queerly. When they asked the girls what was causing their trouble, they all said they didn't know.

The ministers kept right on. Mr. Parris and the Reverend Nicholas Noyes from Salem Town were the worst. They badgered the girls. Something or someone was hurting them. What was it? Was it a person? No one, they all said.

Mr. Parris began to mention the names of those in the village who were considered a little queer, like Sarah Good. At each name the girls shook their heads. And at last the ministers shook theirs and departed.

A little later Mr. Parris suddenly remembered that Betty and Abigail had been spending a good deal of time with Tituba. The minister had seen the other girls at the parsonage more often than usual too. He had been too busy to pay much attention, but now it came back to him with sudden force. He knew about obeah. Tituba . . .

He began to watch the slave. A day or so later he caught her in the kitchen raking something out of the ashes on the hearth. She gave a start as she looked up and saw him, then tossed what she had taken from the fire to the dog, who gulped it down.

"What are you doing, Tituba?" the minister demanded.

"Jus' feed the dog, master," she replied in her soft drawl.

"What did you feed him?"

"Cake, master."

"Cake! What kind of cake?"

Tituba said vaguely that it was "jus' a cake," but Mr. Parris forced her to admit it was a "witch cake." She said she had been so sorry for poor, afflicted little Betty. Witch cakes were unknown in Barbados, but one of the superstitious goodwives of the village had told her how to make one to cure Betty, and she had tried it.

Mr. Parris called Betty into his study and began to question her. What did Tituba talk about when they were together? Charms? Spirits? *Witches* . . . *?* What evil things had she learned from the slave?

The panic-stricken child finally broke down and sobbed out what had happened. With that she went into such violent convulsions that it seemed she would never come out of them. Mr. Parris then had the other girls brought before him and confronted them with what he had discovered. Each one denied that what Betty had said was true.

The minister kept on, asking the same questions over and over, but putting them in a different way each time. Suddenly one of the girls admitted it was all true. With that, the others agreed, one by one.

Mr. Parris still wasn't satisfied. He shot a question at each one in turn: "Who else is in it with Tituba?"

One of the older girls, half sobbing, spoke a name: "Goody Good." Ann Putnam thought of the day she and Mercy Lewis had met Sarah Good on the way to the parsonage. She remembered how the woman had muttered something as they passed. Had it been a curse? When Mr. Parris fixed her with his stern eyes and asked, "Is Sarah Good one of those that hurts you?" she tried not to reply, but in spite of herself she nodded.

"Who else?" The minister had begun his round once more. "Who else afflicts you with Tituba and Goodwife Good?"

A girl spoke up, almost in a whisper: "Goody Osburne."

This did not surprise the minister. For over a year now, Sarah Osburne had not been seen in church on the Sabbath. She was supposed to be ill, but there were those in the congregation who insisted that she was perfectly able to get to the meetinghouse. People were talking, saying there was something queer about it.

Then Mr. Parris asked each of the other girls: "Does Goodwife Osburne hurt you?" All said yes.

Mr. Parris' mouth snapped shut in a thin, grim line. "That will be all for now," he told them.

When they had gone he sent for Tituba. Sure that the slave had much more to tell him, he was determined to have it out of her. When she did not confess, he beat her until she told him just what he wanted to hear.

On the last day of February, warrants were sworn out charging Tituba, Sarah Good and Sarah Osburne with practicing witchcraft. There was no jail in Salem Village, so the constables hauled the three women off to the one in Ipswich. Poor old Goody Osburne was too sick to be put into a foul, cold jail cell, but they took her there, clinging to a pillion on a horse's back behind one of the constables.

An examination was set for the next day. It was to be conducted by two distinguished men of Salem Town, John Hathorne and Jonathan Corwin of the Court of Assistants of Massachusetts Bay. They would decide whether Tituba, Sarah Good and Sarah Osburne must stand trial as accused witches, for which the penalty, as set forth in the Bible, was death.

5

The Three Witches

Tuesday, March 1, 1692, was the greatest day in the history of Salem Village since it had first been settled more than a half century earlier. When Ann Putnam, riding on her pillion behind Mercy Lewis, and Goodwife Putnam on hers behind her husband arrived at the crossroads, an immense throng was milling about the dooryard at Deacon Ingersoll's tavern. After Goodman Putnam had dismounted and helped his wife down, he looked around and shook his head.

"There won't be more than half of 'em that'll be able to squeeze inside," he said. "Looks as if every man, woman and child in Salem Village that can ride or walk is here, not to mention folks from all the towns roundabout."

Ann saw people eyeing her curiously. She felt her cheeks burn. Glancing at Mercy Lewis, she saw that the maidservant's color was high and her eyes bright with excitement, but she didn't meet Ann's eye. She had scarcely said a word all the way to the village center. Here and there Ann picked out some of the other afflicted girls, but they too avoided her gaze.

45

Goodman Putnam, who was the parish clerk, threaded his way through the crowd to the door of the tavern and went inside. Just then Goodwife Pope came up. Like Ann's mother, she had a devouring curiosity about everything that went on in Salem Village. Right now she was fairly bursting with news.

"Did you hear about old Giles Cory?" she demanded of Ann's mother. She was a neighbor of Giles and Martha Cory.

Goodwife Putnam shook her head. "Do tell, Goodwife Pope."

"Why, Giles was fixing to come to the hearings this morning, but Martha wouldn't hear of it. Do you know what Martha done when she first learnt of these poor afflicted children? Laughed."

Goodwife Pope clucked her tongue and her voice as she repeated the word was shrill. "*Laughed!* She'd better have a care . . . Well, Giles said he was going anyhow. Went to saddle his horse and what do you think? Martha'd took the saddle and hid it. That didn't stop Giles, though. He wa'n't going to be done out of coming to town. Rode in without no saddle. Tee! hee!"

She was looking about her. "I see most of the children, all but little Betty Parris."

"Oh, didn't you know?" cried Goodwife Putnam. "Why, the Parrises have sent her away."

"Away!" gasped Goodwife Pope.

Ann's mother nodded solemnly. Now that she had a piece of news she told it with relish. "She's gone to Salem Town to stay with the Stephen Sewalls. Mrs. Parris insisted. She thinks the child couldn't stand being

made to attend the hearings. She believes Betty will get
well if she stays away from all this."

"Fiddlesticks!" snapped Goodwife Pope. "The child's
bewitched, ain't she? Going away'll do her no good. A
witch'll ride to Salem Town on a broomstick quicker'n
you can say it."

Ann saw her father coming from the tavern with Mr.
Parris and some others.

"The magistrates haven't arrived from Salem Town
yet," he told his family. "The constables and some of
the train band have gone to meet them. I'm going over
to the meetinghouse with the minister and the deacons.
They've decided to set the courtroom up there so's more
people can get in."

Behind Mr. Parris and the others, the crowd surged
across the road. A few moments later a beat of drums
was heard from the direction of Salem Town. Then the
magistrates came in sight, flanked by the constables and
with the train band in their wake, all marching to the
roll and slam of the drums. It was something like a train-
ing day when the militia company marched on the
parade ground, though more impressive, with the magistrates in the procession, wearing long black cloaks and
high-crowned hats.

They swung to the right into Meetinghouse Road,
then left and up to the church door, the crowd parting
to let them through. As soon as they had entered the
meetinghouse the rest of the people pressed forward in
a scramble for seats.

Inside, they had moved the pulpit back. A long table,
brought from Ingersoll's, had been set up in its place

for the magistrates and Ezekiel Cheever, Jr., who was to record the proceedings. The minister's big chair had been turned around to form a bar of justice for the prisoners.

The afflicted girls were ushered to the foremost row of benches, right up where everyone could watch them. At the moment, as an expectant hush fell over the meetinghouse, they sat as quietly as if it had been a regular Sabbath service.

Every head turned when a tramp of feet resounded at the entrance in the rear. Constable Locker marched Sarah Good in, his hand gripping her arm tightly. Sarah didn't look frightened. She seemed to be enjoying her notoriety. Dressed in her usual tatters, her hair a rat's nest, she was looking all around her, giving the people bold stare for stare and smirking a little.

They led her to the bar. Once more the spectators sat like graven images as John Hathorne rose from the table and faced her. He was a man with a countenance like a rocky ledge, whose piercing gaze should have cowed Sarah, but didn't.

"Sarah Good, what evil spirit do you have familiarity with?"

"None." She fairly spat the reply in the magistrate's face. Ann Putnam thought of the time her father had shot a hawk that was preying on his chickens. He had brought it down alive, dragging a broken wing. As he came up to shoot again and kill it, it had given him the same fierce look that was in Goody Good's eyes now.

"Have you made no contract with the devil?" Mr. Hathorne continued.

"No."

"Why do you hurt these children?"

"I do not hurt them. I scorn it."

Suddenly Abigail Williams, who was sitting next to Ann Putnam, uttered a shriek and began to writhe in torment. Instantly several of the others did the same. The strange feeling that Ann knew well by this time came over her. Sharp pains darted in her arms and legs, for all the world as if something was pinching cruelly, and she too screamed and writhed.

When Ann's senses returned, the uproar was dying down. Mr. Hathorne was standing there waiting, his eyes fixed on Goody Good. When all was quiet he went on.

"Who do you employ, then, to hurt the children?"

"I employ nobody," Sarah snapped.

Mr. Hathorne asked several other questions, trying in vain to get her to admit she had made a contract with the devil. Then he turned to the girls, sitting quietly now on their benches.

"Look upon her, children, and see if this is the person that hurts you," he said.

A girl shrieked, "Yes, it is Goody Good that hurts me!" The others took up the cry. Ann too screamed that Sarah was hurting her.

"Sarah Good," said Mr. Hathorne sternly when quiet was restored, "do you not see what you have done? Why do you not tell the truth? Why do you thus torment these poor children?"

She turned a scowling, sullen glare upon the magistrate. "I do not torment them."

At the long table, Ezekiel Cheever, Jr., scribbled furiously to get all the words down as Mr. Hathorne continued to badger Sarah Good. Mr. Corwin, the other magistrate, was also taking notes. He was a quiet-looking man with none of Mr. Hathorne's grimness.

At last, unable to force Sarah Good to admit she had hurt the girls, Mr. Hathorne tried a new line of questioning. "Who was it, then, that tormented the children?"

Before she replied, Goody Good looked from one to another in the audience as if searching for a victim. But when she spoke it was to name one of the other prisoners.

"It was Osburne," she rasped. The meetinghouse buzzed as people turned to each other with low-voiced exclamations.

Then the magistrate began to hammer at her again, trying to force something from her that would connect her with witchcraft. When he asked what she muttered when she was turned away from a house, she said it was the commandments. "I may say some commandments, I hope," she added righteously.

When he wanted to know which of the commandments they were, she changed her mind and said it was a psalm. But all she could repeat of it was, "I serve God."

Then Samuel Abbey and his wife testified against Goody Good. The Abbeys had taken Sarah into their home, only to be repaid with such spite and malice that they had had to turn her out again. Later, seventeen head of the Abbeys' cattle had died, as well as sheep and hogs.

They described how Sarah's shiftless husband Wil-

liam had told them that when he spoke to his wife of
the lost cattle, she said she didn't care if Goodman
Abbey lost his whole herd. Goody Good had more than
once threatened their children too, and called them vile
names. Nothing was said about how children sometimes
hooted at Sarah Good and shouted unkind things at her.

The suspicion that Sarah carried smallpox came up
too. Goodwife Sarah Gadge reported she and her husband had turned Sarah Good away during the epidemic
in fear she would bring the disease upon them. Goody
Good had gone off muttering. Next morning one of
their cows had died suddenly. Others told of threats she
had made when refused shelter.

At last Mr. Hathorne sat down. He and Jonathan
Corwin put their heads together and talked in whispers
for a time. Then Hathorne rose and said it was the
magistrates' judgment that Sarah Good be held in jail
to await trial as a witch. Among the spectators, heads
nodded wisely . . .

The hearings continued for five days. It was fortunate
that less work had to be done on the farms of Salem
Village at this season, for scarcely anyone did a lick of
it during the sessions.

Tituba was questioned for three days. So many spectators pushed and shoved their way into the meetinghouse that it seemed its walls would surely burst right
at the seams. They gaped at the slave, with her wild
black hair and glittering black eyes, and her soft voice,
which seemed to carry some devilish allurement.

For a short time Tituba denied everything, but gradually she began to admit all that Mr. Hathorne wanted

her to and more. She had already learned that doing
so with Mr. Parris had caused him to stop whipping
her. Now she told things that left the spectators fairly
drooling in wonder and awe.

When the magistrate asked why she hurt the children, Tituba denied it, but when he asked who did hurt
them, she said, "The devil, for aught I know."

"Did you ever see the devil?" Hathorne demanded.

At Tituba's reply a tremendous gasp went up from
those present: "The devil come to see me and bid me
serve him." Then she said she had seen four women tormenting the children. Two were Sarah Good and Sarah
Osburne; the others she did not know. Oh, yes, and
there was a tall man of Boston.

The jaws of those in the meetinghouse sagged. Was
it possible that Satan was sending witches all the way
from Boston to torment the children? A tall man . . .
who could he be?

The people's jaws seemed in danger of dropping right
into their laps at Mr. Hathorne's next question and
Tituba's reply.

"When did you see them?"

"Last night, at Boston."

Boston! But Tituba had been in Ipswich jail last night,
securely chained and carefully watched. Even if she
could have escaped, it would have taken her several
hours to ride to Boston and back again, assuming she
could get a horse. Surely her absence would have been
discovered unless . . . unless some unearthly means of
transportation had taken her there and back in a twin-
kling . . . a broomstick, perhaps . . .

"What did the ones you saw in Boston say to you?" Mr. Hathorne continued.

"They say hurt the children."

"And did you hurt them?"

Again Tituba denied it, saying it was the four women and one man, but she added that they threatened to hurt her if she did not obey them. And in the next breath she admitted she had hurt the children, but said she was sorry and would do it no more.

Under the magistrate's questioning, Tituba told of seeing an "appearance" four times and that it said to kill the children.

What sort of an appearance? Mr. Hathorne wanted to know.

"Sometimes like a hog and sometimes like a great dog."

"What did it say to you?"

"It say the black dog would serve me. I say I am afraid. It say if I do not, it would do worse to me."

"What did you say to it?"

"I will serve you no longer. Then it say it would hurt me, and then it look like a man and threaten to hurt me."

Mr. Hathorne waited, and when Tituba spoke again it caused a sensation in the meetinghouse. The slave said that the tall man had had a yellow bird. He told her he had more pretty things to give her if she would serve him. As everyone knew, this was exactly the way the devil would tempt a woman to sell him her soul.

Once Tituba was well started on her confession, she told things that set the people by the ears. She had seen other animals, a red rat and a black rat which demanded that she serve them and hurt the children. Worse than that, the four women and the man had taken her to Thomas Putnam's house and tried to make her kill Ann with a knife. They threatened to cut off her head if she refused.

It was plain that none of the people there in the meetinghouse doubted it. They swallowed Tituba's wonderful nonsense and believed.

"How did you go to Putnam's?" Mr. Hathorne asked.

"We ride upon broomsticks and are there presently."

There was much nodding of heads at this response, a kind of silent "I told you so."

There was more, much more. In the "appearance" the slave had seen, Sarah Good had a yellow bird between her fingers. As for Sarah Osburne, she had a yellow dog with the head of a woman, two legs and two wings. Tituba claimed that Abigail Williams had seen it too, and that it turned into the shape of Sarah Osburne. The slave had also seen Sarah Good set a wolf on Elizabeth Hubbard. Goody Good had a cat as well.

Those in the meetinghouse drew in their breaths at that. Everyone knew the devil could not work directly with a witch, but must do so through her familiar. A familiar might be a dog, a toad, a bat, a bird or some other creature, but cats were Satan's favorite.

The magistrates committed Tituba to jail to await trial. She did not seem to mind. In jail, at least, she would not have to work. It was plain that she had had a wonderful time in the meetinghouse, with all the people hanging on every word she had said, and the two magistrates never doubting anything. Although Tituba had told so much that all were sure she was a witch, she didn't seem worried.

The two constables had to support Sarah Osburne when they brought her in, and she leaned on the back of the minister's chair to keep from toppling over. But she faced right up to John Hathorne with a kind of sureness, as though her innocence bore her up.

She denied knowing evil spirits, having a contract with the devil, hurting the children or employing any-one to do so. When Hathorne revealed that Sarah Good had accused her of tormenting the girls, she replied, calmly, "I do not know that the devil goes about in my likeness to do any hurt."

The magistrate then ordered the girls to stand up and look at her. "Do you know this woman?" he asked. When he reached Ann Putnam, uneasiness was making her feel sick to her stomach, but she did as the others had and nodded.

"Is this one of the women that doth afflict you?" Hathorne asked then. Again all nodded.

At last Sarah Osburne admitted she had once had a strange experience. "I was frighted one time in my sleep and I saw or dreamt I saw a thing like an Indian, all black. It pulled me to the door of my house by the neck and the back part of my head."

In a flash Hathorne followed up his advantage. "What did it propose to you?"

"That I should go no more to meeting," she admitted, but added quickly, "I said I would, and did go next Sabbath Day."

He had her trapped now. "Why did you yield so far to the devil as never to go to meeting after that?"

"Alas!" the unhappy creature cried, "I have been sick and unable to go."

Mr. Hathorne turned to the spectators with a knowing look, as much as to say, "You see, her brazen denials have done her no good, for I have got her at last."

He and Mr. Corwin then conferred and announced that in their judgment Sarah Osburne must be tried as a witch. She was taken away, and with that the hearings ended.

That was on Saturday, March 5. On Monday the three accused witches were taken to the jail in Boston. It was a massive, gloomy pile with thick stone walls and dungeons from which no one could escape—no earthly persons, at least.

Salem Village breathed more freely. With three witches (no one thought of them merely as accused persons) securely locked up—and chained up—in Boston Prison, it seemed that the girls' affliction might come to an end. Perhaps the trouble was over.

6

"Everybody Knows There's Witches"

Fog had pulled a vast, dingy blanket over London when Sir William Phips left his lodgings at the Bell Tavern in Holborn one day in April, 1692. It was early afternoon, but it might as well have been midnight. Above Phips' head the wooden galleries surrounding the outside of the ancient inn were lost in the swirling, grimy pall of the fog mingled with the smoke of the great city.

There was a sailor's roll in Phips' walk as he strode through the inn's ponderous gateway. In the street he stopped, peering up and down.

Out of the gloom came a voice: "Chair, sir? 'Ere you are, sir!"

A man like Phips got prompt service in London. He wore a coat and knee breeches of blue velvet, a long-skirted, embroidered waistcoat, white silk stockings and shoes with bows and silver buckles. His hat was as broad of brim and high of crown as that of any London dandy; under it the glossy black curls of an enormous wig fell to his shoulders. [The jeweled scabbard in which his

58

great sword was sheathed would have flashed in the sun had there been any.] Here, it was easy to see, was a man of consequence.

Indeed, the chairmen between the shafts of the sedan chair quickened their pace to a trot once they could make out Phips' resplendent figure clearly. As they halted alongside him, one cried, "A link 'ere, for 'is Worship!"

The dirty yellow flare of a torch loomed out of the murk. On such a day as this there was a link-boy on almost every corner, ready to walk ahead of a hackney coach or sedan chair and guide it to its destination.

Phips got into the chair and gave an order: "Locket's."

It seemed that the two scrawny chairmen would never be able to lift such a bulky, muscular burden, but they were wiry and tough. With the link-boy's torch as a dim beacon ahead of them, they made their way through narrow, crooked streets toward Charing Cross.

In the chair, Phips leaned back, though he did not really relax. He still wasn't used to this ease, luxury and fame that were his. More than once, in the five years since he had brought up a sunken Spanish galleon's fabulous treasure from the sea off the island of Hispaniola, he had felt inclined to pinch himself to make sure it was all true.

He was a rich man. He had heard the streets of this very city resound to wild cheers when he returned from his successful treasure hunt. At Windsor Castle, King James II's sword had touched his shoulder as he was dubbed Sir William Phips, Knight. And now he was to be royal governor of Massachusetts Bay. Could this be the boy who had grown up in grinding poverty on the coast of Maine?

The sedan chair drew up in front of Locket's and Phips entered the famous restaurant. Its paneling of fine wood was carved and gilded, and it glowed with candle-light. It had a quiet elegance; waiters hovered about soundlessly and even the strains of a stringed orchestra were muted and unobtrusive.

Phips' dinner companion was already there and seated. The big man hailed him: "Ahoy, Parson Mather!" The booming voice shattered the quiet of Locket's, a voice pitched to be heard above the blast of a hurricane, the voice of one accustomed to being obeyed.

The Reverend Increase Mather rose with his hand outstretched to greet Phips. They made an odd-looking pair—the Puritan minister in his black robes and the hulking Phips in his gorgeous trappings.

Strange too was the intimacy which had grown up between them. Phips was all sailorman, used to the rough life of a ship's captain and to ruling with an iron hand over crews who were little better than pirates, as indeed some of them had been. Mather, on the other hand, was a learned scholar, a graduate of Harvard College and now its president. Yet the best of friends they were, and the friendship had proved to be of the greatest advantage for Phips.

"Ah, Your Excellency," said Mather, "it is a pleasure to see you, as always, and to dine with you."

Phips beamed. When the two met, his friend always greeted him with his new title, although in ordinary conversation Mather was in the habit of calling him William. It was flattering and the new governor was grateful.

"What news, Parson?" he asked as he seated himself.

"Splendid news, William. The *Nonesuch* is to sail three days hence."

"Good!" shouted Phips. "Give us a fair slatch of wind and we'll soon be in Boston. Ha! there's those that looked down their noses at me that'll find 'em out of joint, mark you. They'll dare not snub me now, and as for their wives that looked down *their* noses at Mary, they'll be quick enough to drop her a curtsy, eh?"

He saw Increase Mather smile. Phips had not been popular with the rich merchants of Boston and their wives, who considered him an upstart. The town had gotten thoroughly sick of him when his ship had stopped there en route to the Bahama Islands on the second of his three voyages in search of treasure. His crew had been a brawling lot, and he himself had been involved in one of their riots. The magistrates had thrown him and his men into jail and released them only when they promised to sail at once for their destination.

Even after he had found and recovered the treasure, Boston had not paid him the homage he expected when he returned with his title and a royal appointment as high sheriff of Massachusetts Bay. He was thirsting for revenge upon those who had sneered at him and his wife, Lady Mary. Now his black eyes burned, betraying his quick temper.

Increase Mather surveyed his friend gravely. There was little of Puritan sternness in the minister's face. His mouth, below a high forehead and rather large straight nose, was kindly but firm. He had the look of a man who would always be just in what his conscience told him was right.

"I well understand your feelings, William," he said, "but as governor you must not forget your dignity."

"Aye," replied Phips, "I make no doubt you're right, Parson. But they'd ought to give us a proper welcome. After all, they're rid of Andros and they must know I won't treat 'em as he did. And they've got you to thank for the new charter."

"I hope they are not disappointed," said Mather. "The new charter is not all I had hoped for, as you know, yet it is a gain for our freedom-loving people. In time we may obtain further liberties."

For years, under a royal charter, Massachusetts Bay had governed itself, choosing its governors and its representatives to the General Court, which enacted the colony's laws. Then King Charles II, deciding that Massachusetts Bay enjoyed altogether too much freedom, had revoked it. His successor, James II, sent a tyranical governor, Sir Edmund Andros, to Boston to rule over all of New England.

At last the people of Massachusetts Bay rose against Andros. They seized and threw him in jail and then sent him to England, asking that he be tried for his despotic acts. They also sent three agents to England, to negotiate for a new charter. One was Increase Mather, for he was not only the most distinguished minister in Boston, but also had great abilities as a statesman.

James II, a despot himself, was not inclined to grant

the new charter, but while Mather and his colleagues were in England the people there rebelled and ousted the King from his throne. William of Orange and his Queen, Mary, then came from Holland to rule England.

William and Mary granted a new charter, but as Mather had just reminded Phips, it was not as liberal as he had hoped. Under it, the governor would be appointed by the King and could disapprove any law passed by the General Court.

Mather pleaded strongly with William and Mary to change their decision. At last they made a concession: they would appoint the governor, but he would be a man recommended by the three agents from Massachusetts Bay.

This was the reason Sir William Phips had obtained the post of royal governor. Mather was the leader and most influential of the agents with William and Mary. He had recommended his friend to them.

As they dined, the two men continued to discuss their plans for returning to Boston. For a first course, Phips attacked roast ribs of beef, an eel pie, a venison pasty and a dish of roasted pigeons. Increase Mather, not being of his friend's size, contented himself with a fricassee of chicken and a hot jowl of salmon.

"By the bye, William," said Mather, "I have another piece of news. You may have a pressing problem to solve when we reach Boston."

Phips' mouth was full of eel pie and it was some moments before he could reply, "What's that, Parson?"

"The ship which arrived yesterday from Boston

brought a letter from my son. There is trouble with witchcraft in Massachusetts Bay."

"Why," said Phips, "that's no news, Parson. They've had trouble aplenty with witches afore this. While I was high sheriff, Goody Glover was hanged for a witch. There'd been others too."

"Ah, yes, a strange case," replied Mather. "You may recall it began when the Goodwin children were tormented. Cotton investigated it, and took the oldest girl into his own home to observe her strange behavior. It is said her fits ceased once Witch Glover was executed."

He was speaking of his son. Cotton Mather was almost as famous a minister as his father, and had made extensive studies of witchcraft.

"I fear this is more serious, however," Increase Mather went on. "A veritable plague of witches has fallen upon the colony. It began in Salem Village, in much the same fashion as the Glover case. Some children are being tormented by witches. The plague is spreading rapidly. Cotton tells me the jail in Salem Town and the prison in Boston are filled with persons accused of witchcraft. It is believed that not all the witches have yet been discovered."

"I'll stop it," Phips declared. "If there's witchcraft afoot, I'll see every witch hunted down and destroyed."

"Yes, that is your duty, William, just as Moses was ordered by God not to suffer a witch to live. But perhaps it is not as simple as it seems. I shall talk to Cotton as soon as we arrive in Boston. He is more familiar with witchcraft than I. But I am disturbed over some of the methods which are used in detecting witches . . ."

"How's that, Parson?"

"For one thing, I do not approve of swimming an accused witch. Persons proved innocent by it often drown. And there are other tests I feel are unreliable and unfair, though there are plenty of sound proofs of witchcraft."

Phips was still hungry. He summoned the waiter. "Fetch me a tansy," he ordered. "You'll join me, Parson?"

"No," said Mather, smiling. "You have more space to fill than I, William."

The tansy, a kind of omelet made with eggs, cream, sugar, rose water and the juices of tansy and other herbs, baked with butter, was set before Phips. He tasted it and smacked his lips.

"Now, there's a dish," he declared. "They don't make 'em in Boston, more's the pity."

Mather was not yet finished with the subject they had been discussing. "I don't want you to think I doubt for a moment that witchcraft prevails," he went on. "It is a dangerous evil which must be stamped out. I take it we're agreed on that?"

Phips nodded. "Of course, Parson. Everybody knows there's witches."

He would not have thought of disagreeing with his benefactor. Phips had an uneducated man's respect for Increase Mather's vast learning. He wondered what the minister would think if he knew the next governor of Massachusetts Bay had never been inside a school. Such learning as he had he had gotten by himself. How could he doubt a scholar who was sure that witchcraft existed?

Besides, he had been brought up to believe in strange happenings, witches and other spirits. No people were more superstitious than the inhabitants of Montsweag, on the coast of Maine, where he had been born.

Phips wondered too what the minister would think if he knew the legend of Montsweag. His mother had had an unbelievable brood of twenty-six children, and he had been her twenty-first son. That, in the minds of the ignorant farmers and fishermen of the poverty-stricken little hamlet, was a lucky number.

"Willie Phips is touched with magic," they said. "He will stand before kings."

It had come true. Phips had stood before three kings and one queen.

When his first voyage after treasure had failed, he had gone to England. There he managed to make influential friends who arranged an audience with Charles II. He had obtained the King's promise of a better ship and equipment for a second voyage.

That venture too had failed. Undaunted, Phips went back to England and sought the aid of James II, who had come to the throne in the meantime. The result was his third and successful quest for a treasure-laden Spanish galleon.

Finally, Phips had come to England on a different mission. From Massachusetts Bay he had led an expedition against the French in Canada. He had tried and failed to capture the mighty stronghold of Quebec. But Phips was never a man to give up anything he had begun. From William and Mary he sought approval of a second attempt to take Quebec, since England and

France were still at war in the first of the long series of conflicts known in America as the colonial wars.

Standing with Increase Mather before this third king and his queen, Phips had been denied what he sought. But due to Mather's favor he had gained the post as royal governor that would make him the most powerful man in Massachusetts Bay.

Phips was almost on the point of telling Increase Mather that he himself was touched with magic, but he thought better of it. The minister might suspect him of powers that were more than earthly . . .

The meal was nearing its end. Phips helped himself to a slice of cheesecake, a tart and a custard from a platter of desserts. Increase Mather had a tart. And with that the two departed to make their final preparations for the voyage to Massachusetts Bay, which was reeling under the curse of its plague of witches.

7

The Plague Spreads

Meanwhile, in Salem Village, putting Tituba, Sarah Good and Sarah Osburne in jail had not stopped the afflicted girls' torments. If anything, they were worse than before. People came in droves to watch them.

Then Ann Putnam cried out on Martha Cory. Goodwife Pope had known what she was talking about when she said Martha had better have a care. People had not forgotten she had laughed at the girls' afflictions and tried to keep her husband from attending the examinations. Although she was a faithful church member and was considered a good woman in spite of her sharp tongue, she was arrested and taken to jail.

Then came a much greater shock to the inhabitants of Salem Village. Another of the former ministers of Salem Village, Deodat Lawson, arrived to investigate the witchcraft trouble. When he went to the parsonage, Abigail Williams had a terrible fit. She seized flaming brands from the fire and hurled them about; then, flapping her arms like wings, she tried to fly up the chimney. She became quiet at last, but suddenly she shrieked that there was a "shape" in the room.

"Do you not see her?" she cried. "Why, there she stands!" She raised her hands and tried to push something away. "I won't!" she screeched. "I won't! I am sure it is none of God's book! It is the devil's book for aught I know!"

"Who is it?" Mr. Lawson asked. "Tell us, child, who is it you see?"

"It is Goody Nurse!"

Mr. Lawson looked at Abigail with stricken eyes. He knew very well there was no finer woman in Salem Village than Rebecca Nurse. She was pious, deeply devoted to her religon, a member of the village church ever since the first one had been erected in 1673. And she was a loving mother who had raised four sons and four daughters. Now she was old and deaf, and for some days had been quite ill.

Then Mr. Parris told Deodat Lawson how the other girls had cried out on Rebecca Nurse. Ann Putnam had begun it, though she had hesitated over her charge. There had been a good many who thought she must be wrong. Yet how could it be doubted when all the afflicted ones said it was so?

Rebecca Nurse was arrested and held in jail to await her examination.

One of the very few in Salem Village who had the courage to speak out about it was John Procter. He was a giant of a man who never hesitated to do what his conscience told him was right. When he heard that his servant girl, Mary Warren, had joined the others in crying out upon Rebecca Nurse, he seized Mary roughly and plumped her down at the spinning wheel.

"Now!" he roared. "You sit there and don't you stir from that wheel, fits or no fits, or I'll give you a thrashing you'll never forget!"

It cured Mary for a while, but then the magistrates sent for her to testify at the hearings. John Procter objected, but he could not stand against their authority, and Mary Warren's affliction returned. The other girls, hearing what had happened, did not forget John Procter.

Another fearless one was Joseph Putnam, one of Ann's uncles. He was a young man who would later raise a family of thirteen children. The twelfth of them, Israel Putnam, would inherit his father's courage and become a famous fighter in the Indian wars and a hero of the battle of Bunker Hill in the Revolution.

One day the door of Thomas Putnam's house burst open and Joseph Putnam stomped in. He went up to Ann's mother. "If you dare touch with your foul lies anyone belonging to my household, you shall answer for it!" he thundered.

Then he went back to his farm, loaded his musket and saddled a horse. He kept both the gun and the animal in readiness as long as the witchcraft delusion lasted.

Ann and her mother knew he meant every word of what he said. So did the other afflicted girls when they heard of it. No one ever cried out upon Joseph Putnam or any of his family.

Martha Cory showed great courage too when her examination was held on March 21. It was a battle between her and John Hathorne from start to finish.

The magistrate went for her with tigerish ferocity.

But try as he would, he could not make her admit she had any connection with witchcraft.

Everything seemed to go against her, however. Perhaps her husband was still smarting because she had hidden his saddle, for he gave hostile testimony against her. So did one of her sons-in-law.

When the long examination was over, Martha flung one last defiance at the magistrates: "You can't prove me a witch!" But whether they could or not, they marched her off to jail in Salem Town. She went with her head still high. They had not made her confess, in the hope of mercy, to something she had not done.

Then came Rebecca Nurse's examination. The wretched, frail old creature, who had been wrenched from her sick bed and thrown into jail, leaned on the minister's chair, so weak she could hardly stand to be questioned. She faced the people in her decent gray gown with its white kerchief at the neck and her white-winged Puritan cap, looking about in desperation for one face in which she could find some hope.

Before Rebecca's ordeal was over, many of those in the meetinghouse were weeping. Even the relentless John Hathorne's manner was mild when he began the questioning. In his mind, as well as in the minds of the spectators, there was doubt.

But there was mischief afoot that day of March 23. Even this inoffensive goodwife had her enemies in Salem Village, not because she had ever done anyone any harm, but because the Nurse family had prospered.

Francis and Rebecca Nurse and their sons and daughters had done well on the fine, three-hundred-acre farm with its sturdy farmhouse which they had bought fourteen years before. But vindictive people in Salem Village who begrudged the Nurse family its success had no pity for Rebecca. During the examination a number of them testified about queer things they had seen her do or had heard she had done.

Perhaps Mr. Hathorne thought the sight of the forlorn old woman might cause the afflicted girls to change their minds. Instead of questioning Rebecca immediately when the examination began, he turned to Abigail Williams.

"Abigail, have you been hurt by this woman?"

"Yes," the little girl replied.

Before the magistrate could ask Ann Putnam the same question, she fell in a fit, crying out that Rebecca was hurting her. Hathorne turned to the old woman. "Goody Nurse, what do you say to it?"

Rebecca lifted her eyes to heaven. "I can say before my eternal Father, I am innocent, and God will clear my innocence."

"There is never one in the assembly but desires it," Hathorne said gently, "but if you be guilty, pray God discover you."

A moment later a woman's shrill voice rose above the bedlam in the room. "Did you not bring the Black Man with you? Did you not bid me tempt God and die?"

It was Ann Putnam's mother. A day or so before, she had joined the girls in accusing Rebecca. She claimed the old woman's shape had tempted her to evil and had hurt her when she refused.

"What do you say to this?" Hathorne asked.

Rebecca thrust out her hands in utter helplessness. "Oh, Lord, help me!" she cried.

Then the magistrate took up a paper and read from it. This was another charge Goodwife Putnam had made. Little children wearing the winding sheets in which they had been buried had appeared to her. Witch Nurse had murdered them, they said.

The people in the meetinghouse held their breaths. Could it be that this innocent-looking old woman was a bloody-handed murderess?

By the time Hathorne and her accusers were through with her, the spectators were convinced that, in spite of all their doubts, Rebecca Nurse must be a witch. At last it was over, and they took the miserable old soul off to jail in Salem Town to await her trial.

There still remained one "witch" to be brought before the magistrates. When Hathorne read the charge against her she simply stood there, small, helpless, bewildered, frightened. Then they took her off to Boston Prison and chained her up with her mother.

She was Dorcas Good, one of Sarah Good's brood, accused by Ann Putnam. Dorcas was five years old.

Next the girls turned their spite against Rebecca Nurse's sister, Sarah Cloyce. Sarah was incensed at what had been done to Rebecca. When Mr. Parris preached about witchcraft one Sunday, demanding that every witch be destroyed, Sarah got up, white-faced and trembling, stalked down the aisle and left the church, slamming the door behind her.

The girls charged that Sarah had gone from the

church straight to Mr. Parris' nearby pasture. There, they said, were witches, a whole black flock of them, celebrating their own Sabbath.

Sarah Cloyce was arrested and held for an examination.

The girls may have been a little afraid of John Procter, who had threatened Mary Warren with a whipping. They did not accuse him, but they vented their spite by crying out on his wife, Elizabeth. They claimed she had been with Goody Cloyce at the witches' Sabbath in Mr. Parris' pasture.

The plague of witches in little Salem Village had caused such a sensation in Massachusetts Bay that it was decided to hold the next hearings in the larger meeting-house in Salem Town. No less a personage than the deputy governor of the province, Thomas Danforth, was to preside, assisted by five members of the governor's Council.

The six stern-faced men were tremendously dignified in long black robes, with white stocks at their throats and black skullcaps on their heads. The afflicted girls may have feared these judges would stand for none of the nonsense the magistrates had been so quick to believe. But it was plain from the start that the only nonsense they would not stand for was from the accused witches.

They called John Indian as a witness against Sarah Cloyce. Tituba's husband had decided it was wiser to be bewitched himself than to be charged with witchcraft like his wife. He told so many fantastic tales about

Sarah Cloyce that she shouted at him: "Oh, you are a grievous liar!"

When Elizabeth Procter faced her accusers, John Procter stood up and defended his wife loyally. The girls, sure now that the judges were on their side, made such an uproar that Procter had to shout to make himself heard.

Then Abigail Williams shrieked, "Why, he can pinch as well as she!" Another girl cried out that he was "a most dreadful wizard."

Mr. Danforth wasted no more time on them. He packed both Elizabeth and John Procter, along with Sarah Cloyce, off to Boston Prison.

Mary Warren was not present that day. Either because John Procter had so frightened her or for some other reason, she had suddenly decided she had been wrong in crying out upon the accused witches.

The other girls found out about it. "She's trying to back out, the jade!" Mercy Lewis muttered. "She's telling people the rest of us lied about the witches! We'll fix her clock!"

Fix it they did. They cried out on Mary and on April 12 she was arrested and brought into court, now restored to Salem Village, before Hathorne and Corwin.

There she cried out, "Oh, I am sorry for it! Oh, Lord, help me! Oh, good Lord, save me! I will tell! I will tell!" Then she sank into a trance, her jaws locked so that she could speak no more.

Perhaps the magistrates were worried lest Mary's confession might bring the whole witchcraft affair tumbling about their ears, along with the blame for listening to the girls' charges. They had her carried to jail before she could tell what she had threatened to reveal.

The plague of witches was now spreading like a fire through tinder-dry woods. It had fallen upon several villages in the countryside surrounding Salem Village.

On the day Mary Warren was arrested, three others were brought before the magistrates. They were Bridget Bishop, Abigail Hobbs and Martha Cory's husband, Giles.

Bridget Bishop ran a tavern on the road between Salem Town and Beverly which had an unsavory reputation. As for Abigail Hobbs of Topsfield, she was a wild, gypsylike creature, fond of roaming the woods at night, for what purpose Satan alone knew. She not only cheerfully admitted she was a witch, but accused several others, including her own father and mother.

Giles Cory had been in trouble with the law before and had many enemies. No one spoke up for him before the magistrates, but he had an iron will and was afraid of nothing. He sought no mercy by confessing.

The magistrates sent all three to jail. The next day there were seven more persons, among them Abigail Hobbs' parents. Six were committed to prison.

The seventh prisoner was Nehemiah Abbott. He was a very old man, almost a hundred, he claimed. When Mr. Hathorne asked the girls if he hurt them, Mercy Lewis spoke up positively: "He is not the man."

Ann Putnam, sitting with the others, gasped. Mercy was one of the vindictive ones. Some of the rest demanded to be allowed to search Nehemiah Abbott for a witch mark.

Everyone knew the one sure way to tell a witch or a wizard was by a witch mark. It could be a small red spot like an insect bite, a little mole, wart or discolored place on the skin. Often people saw in a witch mark the shape of a familiar—a toad, bat, spider or frog. But the girls found no witch mark on Nehemiah Abbott.

Mr. Hathorne discharged him—the first of the accused witches to go free. Ann Putnam, knowing Mercy Lewis' sly ways, wondered if the girl had failed on purpose to identify Nehemiah as a wizard. Didn't his release prove the examinations were fair? Didn't it show that anyone who was innocent had nothing to fear?

The girls were not finished with Rebecca Nurse's family. Next they cried out on Mary Esty, another of Rebecca's sisters. She was known to everyone as a saintly woman, and she bore herself with serene and sweet dignity when she faced Mr. Hathorne. But she too was sent to jail.

Then came Susanna Martin of Amesbury. She was the one whose friend in Newbury charged she had flown there on a broomstick. Susanna was not liked in Amesbury, and several witnesses told of strange things she had done.

Susanna was put in prison. So was dignified Dorcas Hoar of Beverly, a widow. The girls charged she had murdered her husband.

Of all the sensations that had rocked Salem Village since the beginning of the witchcraft troubles, the most shocking of all lay just ahead. In Salem Town, the magistrates received a letter from Ann Putnam's father with a staggering disclosure.

Ann had been seized with a fit near Mr. Parris' pasture. "Oh, dreadful, dreadful!" she cried out. "Here is a minister come! What! are ministers witches too?"

It was a witches' Sabbath in Mr. Parris' pasture that she saw. Among them, she told her father, was "a little black minister that lives at Casco Bay."

The little minister, hearing her, had set upon and tormented her, then coaxed her to write in his book.

"It is a dreadful thing that you, a minister, that should teach children to fear God, should come to persuade poor creatures to give their souls to the devil," she reproached him. "Oh, dreadful, dreadful! Tell me your name that I may know who you are."

He did tell her, adding that he had murdered three wives, two of his own and one of Deodat Lawson's. When Ann repeated his name to her father, he shuddered. Later, at home, Goodwife Putnam had not seemed surprised. She said she had suspected him for years.

Casco Bay was a long way off in the wilderness of Maine, which was then a part of Massachusetts Bay. The little settlement of Wells was in the region. Its settlers struggled to eke out a precarious existence by fishing, hunting and raising corn, beans and flax, hewing wood to take them through the terrible winters. They lived in constant terror of the Indians and their French allies in Canada.

The minister in Wells, George Burroughs, was a short man of very dark complexion, with black hair and eyes. He had married again after his second wife died. With the new one, a widow who had a daughter, and his own seven children, he lived contentedly in Wells. He was a farmer during the week and a preacher on the Sabbath, bringing the word of God to the settlers. In spite of the danger from the French and Indians, it was far better than when he had been the minister in Salem Village. There he had had nothing but trouble and persecution.

Spring had come to Maine. The trees and shrubs were leafing out. In the damp woods, violets, trillium and bloodroot peeped from beneath the brown carpet of last year's leaves. Birds trilled liquid praises of spring, and the cowslips in the marshy places were like heaps of golden coins flung down by some Midas.

Trout were leaping in the brooks. George Burroughs, as he sat down to dinner at noon with his family, thought he might take a pole and line and catch a mess of them for supper.

Suddenly there came a furious hammering at the door. The minister, always alert for an alarm of an Indian attack, leaped to his feet, strode to the door and flung it open.

A rough-looking man he did not know stood there, holding a musket pointed straight at him. "Are you George Burroughs?" he demanded.

"Yes."

"I'm a constable, John Partridge of Portsmouth. I have a warrant for your arrest."

"Warrant! What—for?"

"Witchcraft. Come along, now."

And with that he hustled the bewildered Burroughs off. He did not even give his prisoner time to pack what he might need for the journey. The minister's dinner remained half eaten on the table, while his wife and children stared after his retreating figure, speechless with shock.

The "little black minister" was on his way to face his accusers of Salem Village, with his life at stake.

Where was it all to end? As the witchcraft delusion spread over an ever larger area outside Salem Village, no one knew. How could it end when there was no one to stop it?

8

The Court of Oyer and Terminer

At the fort on Castle Island in Boston Harbor, late on the afternoon of May 14, 1692, the topsails of a ship were seen coming up over the horizon to the east. A few minutes later her masts, spars and all her white-winged canvas, as well as the outline of her hull, could be made out. A messenger ran to the commander of the fort.

"The *Nonesuch* frigate has been sighted, sir," he announced.

Instantly a boat was rowed ashore to Dorchester, on the mainland. From there a courier galloped through Roxbury into Boston and along the town's crooked streets to Governor Bradstreet's mansion in the fashionable North End.

Venerable Simon Bradstreet heaved a sigh of relief when he heard the news. He was eighty-nine years old and very tired. The arrival of Sir William Phips as royal governor would put an end to Bradstreet's long and distinguished career of public service.

Simon Bradstreet was a wise and benevolent old man, the only one left of the band of venturers who had come

from England in 1630 and settled Boston. He had served
first as secretary of the Bay Colony. Then, in 1679, he
had been elected governor and remained in this office
seven years, beloved by all.

When the people of Massachusetts Bay revolted
against Sir Edmund Andros in 1689, they had set up a
temporary government until the new rulers of England,
William and Mary, should appoint a new governor.
They asked Bradstreet to serve again, and in spite of his
age he consented.

Simon Bradstreet did not like what was going on in
Salem Village. On the day the examinations were held
in Salem Town he would have gone there to see for
himself, but he was too infirm to make the journey. So
he had sent Thomas Danforth in his stead. But he was
still greatly disturbed about the many accused witches
who were in jail.

As the *Nonesuch* hove abreast of Castle Island, Sir
William Phips and Increase Mather were in the bow,
straining their eyes for a first glimpse of Boston. The
spanking breeze, which had bowled the vessel along at a
merry clip until she entered the harbor, had dropped to
the merest breath, and she was now inching along. Over-
head, the sails slatted idly as whatever air they held was
spilled out of them.

"I am afraid, William, that we shall not reach Boston
in time," said Mather.

"We've got to, Parson!" cried Phips. He began to
pace the deck impatiently. At last he growled, "I'll light
a powder train under those lubbers!"

He stormed aft to the quarterdeck, where the captain stood beside the helmsman.

"Clap on more sail!" Phips roared. "Can't you see it's nigh sunset?"

"She's carrying every stitch we can crowd on her, Governor," replied the skipper.

"Then have the yards braced up! You're losing the wind! I could swim and be in Boston afore ye!"

He threw an anxious glance toward the west, where the sun, a red ball, was nearing the horizon. Then, throwing out his hands in a gesture of despair, he strode back to his companion.

He knew what the approach of darkness meant. This was Saturday. In Puritan Boston the Sabbath began at sunset. Not a wheel would turn and no one would go abroad except to church until sunset the next day. There would be no official welcome for the new governor and the colony's envoy to the court of William and Mary. All through the voyage, Phips had dreamed of a monster parade with many marching regiments to escort him to his home.

"Do not be so distraught, William," said Mather. "They'll be none the less glad to see you, I'll warrant."

Night fell before the *Nonesuch* reached Long Wharf at the foot of Boston's King Street. Phips' shoulders sagged, his black eyes lost their sparkle and he looked like anything but the swashbuckling fellow he was.

Then came a miracle. Gazing out over Boston as they began to warp the *Nonesuch* into her moorings, Phips saw that all the houses were illuminated. In every window, candles shed their beams, imparting a soft radiance to the scene.

And when the two men disembarked, a great, silent mass of soldiers was drawn up in ranks along the two-thousand-foot length of Long Wharf. Then, without the usual squealing fifes and rolling drums, eight regiments of militia marched up King Street behind the new governor and the famous minister. There was no sound but the steady tramp of marching feet.

When word of the frigate's approach reached Simon Bradstreet, he had summoned his Council. They decided that because of the tremendous importance of the event and since Increase Mather was a minister, the strict Sabbath law could be relaxed. And for all its hush the parade up King Street, with silent figures jamming the lighted windows, was a far more impressive tribute than the riotous welcome Sir William Phips had hoped for.

The new governor's house was also in the fashionable North End. Before he left on his first expedition, with a Spanish galleon's treasure only a mirage glimmering before him, Phips had promised his wife Mary, "When I come back rich I'll build you a fair brick house in the Green Lane." Now the house stood there, an elegant residence with broad lawns in front and gardens in the rear.

Lady Phips, a woman of great spirit, was waiting to welcome him. She had seen little enough of her husband in the years when he had been off hunting treasure and during his long absences in England. But she had made the best of it, and now that he was governor she hoped he would settle down in Boston for the rest of his life.

Phips found her greatly upset when he arrived home. "Oh, William!" she cried. "A terrible thing has happened. People everywhere are being accused of witchcraft. The jail in Prison Lane is full of the wretched creatures."

"I've heard of it," said Phips. " 'Twould seem that the Old Scratch is up to some very devilish work in Massachusetts Bay."

"I don't believe it!" Lady Mary insisted. "I have heard that many accused witches are in prison because spiteful people have cried out on them."

"Don't worry, my dear. I shall look into it. If innocent people are confined, they will be released."

"I don't believe any of them are witches!" said his wife stoutly.

Phips stared at her incredulously. "Do you presume to contradict men of great learning like Cotton and Increase Mather? They have investigated witchcraft carefully and are sure there are witches. From what Increase Mather tells me, these people have done strange things which can only be explained by their being in league with the devil."

"I only know that something is terribly wrong, William."

On Monday, Phips lost no time in going to the Town House to take over his duties as governor and confer with Simon Bradstreet. Familiar sights and sounds greeted him on every side as his coach lumbered and lurched over the cobblestones.

Boston pulsed and hummed with activity that Monday morning. The Sabbath quiet had vanished. Street peddlers rang their handbells and cried all manner of wares. From within blacksmiths' shops a great clangor came from their anvils, and the fires in the forges glowed like sullen red eyes. Farther away, toward the harbor, Phips could hear a clatter from the shipyards there.

Heavily laden wagons carrying cargo to and from ships, carts from the country piled high with firewood and farm products, chaises and now and then a splendid coach like his own constantly blocked the way. Since there were no sidewalks, pedestrians overflowed into the streets, scattering like gabbling geese before the horses' hoofs. Over the doorways of the many shops were quaint signs showing their trades—the Bible and Heart, a bookseller's; a dyer's shop displaying an aggrieved-looking dog dyed blue; a grocer's bearing the sign of the Three Sugar Loaves.

Phips was pleased with what he saw. Boston was the biggest town in the American colonies, and he was governor of all Massachusetts Bay. An ambitious man like himself could not ask for a better post in Their Majesties' colonial government.

The coach emerged into the town's widest and most impressive thoroughfare, King Street, up which Phips had paraded in triumph on the eve of the Sabbath. At its head stood the Town House, an odd-looking wooden structure built up on stiltlike pillars. The space under it on the ground level was the Exchange, a place where merchants gathered to discuss ships, cargoes and trade in general.

A group of them parted to let Phips through and greeted him respectfully as he descended from the coach and made his way toward the stairs leading to the upper story. Up there in the Council Chamber, Simon Bradstreet, in austere Puritan dress of black silk, was waiting.

He greeted Phips warmly. The new royal governor could not suppress a smile. He was thinking of the time his ship, the *Golden Rose*, had stopped in Boston on his second treasure-hunting voyage, and he had been arrested with his riotous sailors. It had been Bradstreet, as chief magistrate, who had given him a tongue-lashing and threatened to send him to England in chains if he did not leave Boston at once.

Phips had just time enough to present his commission from William and Mary as royal governor, when Bradstreet spoke of what was uppermost in his mind.

"You are aware, I make no doubt, of the witchcraft troubles which have beset the colony, your Excellency?" the aged man asked.

"Aye," said Phips. "Has aught been done to bring these accused persons to trial?"

"Since news of your appointment had been received, and I knew I should leave office soon, it was my judgment that any action should be left to you," Bradstreet replied. "But there are aspects of the matter which disturb me. I am strongly of the mind that the accused witches must be tried promptly—and fairly."

"I'll look into it at once," Phips promised. "I want first to talk to the Mathers about it. They have had much experience with witchcraft, as you know."

Then Bradstreet brought up another subject. "There is trouble of a different sort in Maine," he continued.

"Ha!" cried Phips. "So the French and their Indian friends are up to more deviltry, eh?"

"Aye. In February a war party of Abenakis attacked York and burned it. They were armed by Frontenac."

Phips pricked up his ears. Although his plea to head another expedition against Quebec had been denied by William and Mary, he had not given up all hope of another encounter with the redoubtable Count Frontenac, the French governor of Canada.

"I knew this would happen," he said. "There will never be peace in the Bay Colony until Quebec is taken and the French driven from Canada. Has there been further trouble?"

"No, but the settlers in Maine are greatly alarmed."

"I'll take it up with the Council," said Phips. "It may be necessary to send a force to Maine and show those red fiends we mean business."

Phips found out how the people felt about the witch-craft troubles when he met with his Council. Under the new charter, William and Mary had appointed the members of this first one with the advice of Increase Mather and the other two agents sent to England. It had twenty-eight members. Although the King and Queen could have sent men from England to sit on it, all were from Massachusetts Bay, persons of high standing in the colony.

The Council was a sort of senate, forming the upper house of the General Court. It was to join with the House of Representatives, whose members were elected by the people, in making the colony's laws. It was also to serve in advising the governor.

The subject of witchcraft came up at once. A member cried, "The people live in fear of the witches who are in jail! They demand that all of them be put in irons!"

"Why should they be chained?" asked Phips. "They have not yet been tried. For all we know, some may be innocent."

"They have been examined and proved to be witches," another member retorted. "If they are not chained they may escape and take vengeance upon the people."

Most of the Council agreed. Phips realized how difficult his position was. He felt sure that many of the accused were indeed witches. On the other hand he suspected that others were in jail because of the spite of their enemies. Yet if he failed to act he might be faced with a rebellion by the aroused people in which he would be ousted as Andros had been.

"Very well," he agreed, "I'll order the accused persons put in irons."

This he did, but he followed up his order with a secret one to the jailers: "Remove the chains from the prisoners."

This subterfuge might soon be discovered, he knew. If it were, he would be in even greater trouble. He pondered the question at length and consulted with the Mathers about it.

The two ministers, especially the younger Cotton Mather, were determined that witchcraft must be exterminated in Massachusetts Bay. Nevertheless, they agreed that the prisoners must be brought to trial promptly and given a fair one. Increase Mather repeated his doubts about some of the evidence used in the examinations. Phips should make certain that such evidence was not accepted at the trials.

"I'll see that they get fair ones," Phips declared. "To conduct them I'll appoint a special Court of Oyer and Terminer."

The terms "oyer" and "terminer" come from two words of French origin meaning "to hear" and "to decide." A Court of Oyer and Terminer was one especially created to try cases involving a particular crime. Thus Phips would name the court solely to try the accused witches and decide their fate.

He gave long and thoughtful consideration to those he would appoint as judges. At last he named six men. They were Samuel Sewall, John Richards, William Sergeant and Wait Winthrop of Boston, Nathaniel Saltonstall of Haverhill, and Bartholomew Gedney of Salem Town. In one way or another most had had experience as judges. All were persons of prominence in the colony.

Today the one most remembered is Samuel Sewall. Like the even more famous Samuel Pepys of London, Sewall for more than fifty years kept a diary in which he set down observations about daily life in Massachusetts Bay. To him, more than to any other man, historians are indebted for their knowledge of how people in the colony lived, worked and amused themselves, what they wore and what they ate.

A kindly man, with a quick, active mind, Samuel Sewall was interested in people. He was not at all the kind of judge who would be expected to send poor wretches to the gallows without mercy.

There remained the chief justice of the Court of Oyer and Terminer to be selected. There was little question as to who he should be. The governor of Massachusetts Bay was also its chief magistrate. Who but Sir William Phips should sit as chief justice of this all-important court?

Suddenly something happened which changed Phips' plans. On June 10 four hundred warriors—Micmacs and Abenakis—led by a Frenchman, Baron de Saint-Castine, struck at the little settlement of Wells in Maine.

Some of its inhabitants had fled after the attack on neighboring York in February, but a handful of settlers who remained decided to fight to the last man if need be. They resisted heroically and at last drove the attackers off. But it was plain that help was needed quickly if further raids were to be prevented.

Phips saw the need for prompt action. "I'll send an armed force to Maine to rebuild the fort at Pemaquid," he decided. This coastal stronghold had been destroyed in an attack a few years before. "We'll leave a garrison there to protect the settlements."

Who should lead the expedition? Since Phips had been born and brought up on the coast of Maine, he knew the country perfectly. And he fancied himself a military man of great ability. He had never been satisfied to be known merely as a sea captain and successful treasure hunter.

He still smarted over the memory of his expedition against Quebec. It had been a miserable failure. Phips was desperately anxious to make up for that fiasco. If he could not try again to take Quebec, he might at least restore his military reputation by going himself to Maine and protecting the settlements. But could he go?

His duty, obviously, was to stay in Massachusetts Bay and preside over the Court of Oyer and Terminer. He was needed there to see that innocent persons were not sent to the gallows. And there were able men who could lead the expedition to Maine.

Yet the idea of going in person was tantalizing. At last he yielded to the temptation. Some historians say he did so because he feared to remain and face the witch-craft troubles, but his later actions belie such a thing. And no one has pointed out that the uneducated governor knew little or nothing of the law, and was poorly fitted to sit as a judge.

He called in his lieutenant-governor, William Stoughton. "I must go to Maine in command of the force to put down the French and savages there," he said. "I am appointing you chief justice of the Court of Oyer and Terminer to try the persons accused of witchcraft."

It was a logical thing to do. Stoughton was the second-ranking official in the colony. A distinguished man too, a graduate of both Harvard College and Oxford University, and with a record of long service as a representative in the General Court.

But just to look at William Stoughton was enough to make even a stout heart quail. His face was as long and pale and cold as a marble tombstone. He was sixty years old and rich, sour of temper, and a bachelor, perhaps because his stony heart had never been warmed by love for anyone but himself. A merciless man, vindictive, and so obstinate that once he had made up his mind, nothing could change it.

This was the chief justice of the court which would determine the fate of the miserable men and women locked up in the jails of the colony, accused of witchcraft.

9
Escape

For most of the accused men and women who refused to confess to being witches, there was little enough hope of escaping trial before the Court of Oyer and Terminer. Yet among these stout-hearted ones were a few who found the means of cheating the gallows.

When Philip English took his wife Mary to visit the Parrises in Salem Village one day late in March, 1692, he had not the slightest idea that they were riding into a trap which would soon snap shut and seize both of them in its jaws. If he had, he would never have left her there.

No doubt one reason Mary went was to hear the latest news of the witchcraft troubles. However, the Parrises and the Englishes were old friends. Probably the friendship went back to the time when Mr. Parris was engaged in the Barbados trade, for Philip English was a merchant whose ships also traded with the West Indian island.

After dropping his wife at the parsonage, he started back to Salem Town, promising to return in a day or two. He was too busy to stay, nor did he have as much curiosity as she did about the plague of witches in Salem

Village. Of course, no one in Salem Town could help
knowing about it, but seeing to all the details of his
flourishing business kept him so well occupied that he
had not even had time to attend the examinations of the
accused witches.

Danger was farthest from his thoughts when he set
out to fetch his wife home. As he rode along that day he
was thinking of how good it was to be alive and how
well life had treated him.

Philip English was forty-one years old. He had spent
twenty-two of those years in Salem Town. Until he was
nineteen he had been Philippe Langlois, living on the
English island of Jersey in the English Channel, a few
miles off the coast of France.

His parents were French Huguenots. In the early seventeenth century the Huguenots, who were Protestants,
had been persecuted in Catholic France. Many fled, and
a number came to Jersey. There Philippe Langlois had
been born.

Life had not been as good to him in those early years.
The people of Jersey were poor farmers, fishermen and
sailors. Philippe had followed the seafaring trade. Then,
aboard a ship that touched at Salem Town, he had decided to remain in America.

A merchant there, William Hollingworth, hired
Philippe to work in his countinghouse or office. Because
the people found his name hard to pronounce, he
changed it to Philip English, since the name Langlois
had come from the French word *l'anglais*, meaning "the
Englishman."

Things went well for Philip after that. He lived with

his employer, who thought well of him because he was
a hard worker and quick to learn the merchant's trade.
Philip especially enjoyed being with the Hollingworths
because they had a pretty, vivacious daughter. In 1675,
five years after coming to America, he married Mary
Hollingworth. At about the same time William Hollingworth died while on a trading voyage to Virginia. Philip
took over the business.

Riding toward Salem Village that March day, Philip
English thought of how he had prospered. He was one
of the richest merchants in New England. More than a
score of his ships traded with the West Indies, his native
island of Jersey, and ports in France. He owned a wharf
where his vessels docked in Salem Town, a large ware-
house where cargoes were stored, and a number of other
buildings which brought in profitable rents. Close by the
wharf was his house, which he also used as a countinghouse. It was a showplace, a large, many-gabled dwelling, known as "English's Great House."

As for the witchcraft trouble now spreading so rapidly, Philip English gave little thought to it. Naturally,
like almost everyone else, he did not doubt for a moment
that the plague of witches was real. As to the possibility
that it could ever concern him or his family, he would
have laughed at the very idea. He was not only Salem
Town's richest man and a distinguished citizen, but one
of the selectmen who administered the town's government.

In Salem Village his wife was ready to leave and they
set out at once. Mary English rode on a pillion astride
the horse's back behind her husband.

"Philip," she said as they trotted along, "I am distraught over what I have seen and heard in Salem Village."

"How so, my dear?"

"I believe innocent people are being accused as witches. Something is wrong and I know it."

"What makes you think so?" English asked.

"You know they have poor, feeble old Rebecca Nurse in jail?"

"Aye," said her husband, "I remember hearing she is accused."

"I went to see her sister, Sarah Cloyce, while I was in Salem Village. She's near daft with worry over Rebecca. Oh, Philip! Rebecca Nurse is no more a witch than I am, and I told Sarah so. I think we should do something about it."

For the first time the merchant felt a twinge of alarm. "What can we do?" he asked uneasily.

"Rebecca Nurse needs help to save her life. Surely they will listen to *us* if we speak up for her."

English shook his head. "The magistrates committed Goodwife Nurse to jail. The examination was most thorough, I am told, and she was given every chance to clear herself."

"I don't believe it!" cried Mary English.

Realizing that his wife was greatly agitated, English tried to calm her and to change the subject, but she continued to speak of it.

At last he said brusquely, "There is naught we can do. I am sorry you went to Goodwife Cloyce. It was unwise. In these troubled times it is well to be prudent in speech and action. Let no more be said of this, Mary."

Soon after their return to Salem Town there was trouble for Sarah Cloyce. The girls cried out against her and she was sent to join her sister Rebecca in jail. It made Philip English even more uneasy, but as the days passed and nothing happened, his fears subsided.

Then, toward midnight on April 21, he and his wife were roused from sleep by a furious hammering at their door. He got up, lighted a candle and went downstairs.

"Who is it?" he called out.

"The sheriff. Open up, in the name of the law!"

"What do you want?"

"I have a warrant for the arrest of Mary English."

For a moment Philip English could not speak. Then he demanded hoarsely: "What for?"

"Witchcraft. Open up, I say!"

English threw the door open. He knew the sheriff well, but in the candlelight he could see no friendliness in the officer's face.

"There's some mistake," he muttered. "There *must* be. My *wife* . . . ?"

The sheriff began to read his warrant. As if from a dream, snatches of its quaint phrases penetrated the merchant's ears: ". . . for high suspicion of sundry acts of witchcraft . . . donne upon the bodies of Ann Putnam, Mercy Lewis and Mary Walcott . . ."

Philip English's senses were beginning to clear. In a rage he bellowed: "What do you mean, coming to my house in the dead of night?"

"I must take your wife to jail to await examination," the sheriff replied.

"Get out of my house!" English thundered. "You'll not take her to jail tonight."

The sheriff hesitated. Arresting defenseless old wives of simple farmers was one thing, but Philip English had influence . . .

"Set up a guard over the house," he ordered the deputies who stood behind him. To English he said, "I'll be back first thing in the morning."

When he had gone, English went upstairs to the chamber where his wife was sitting up in bed.

"What is it, Philip?"

He put his arms around her. "Mary, you are accused as a witch."

She uttered a horrified cry. "Whom have I injured? Who has accused me?"

"Some of the girls—those wretched children in Salem Village. They must have heard what you said to Goodwife Cloyce. But don't you worry, Mary. I'll get you out of this."

The Englishes slept no more that night. But when the sheriff returned about dawn, Mary English calmly told her husband, "Let him wait. I do not propose to get up before my usual time."

When they rose, she said, "Wake the children, Philip. I must talk to them."

Her five children ranged from Mary, who was fifteen, down to William and John, who were infants. Around the breakfast table she discussed the future with the older ones.

"Mary," she said to her oldest daughter, "you must take care of the other children and your father for a few

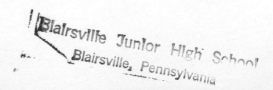

days, since I am going away. If I do not return soon, we will make other arrangements."

What happened from then on has to be gleaned from several accounts which do not agree in all respects. The main facts are known, but there are few details, and some of them are unreliable because they do not bear out the main facts.

Here, pieced together from the more reliable portions of the accounts, is one version of the Englishes' escape.

Mary English was taken to the jail in Salem Town to await her examination. Her husband immediately began to use all his considerable influence to have her released. Finding this impossible, he turned his attention toward getting her transferred to the prison in Boston, which was somewhat less crowded than the little building in Salem Town.

Susanna Sheldon was the chief witness against Mary English. She charged that the merchant's wife had visited her three times and tempted her. Once Mary had come with Martha and Giles Cory. They tried to make Susanna take the devil's book, but she refused it. "Then," she swore, "they did all bite me and went away."

Mrs. English was sent back to jail to await trial.

Then Philip English was warned that he too was in trouble. On April 30 a warrant for his arrest was issued in Salem Town.

The settlement of Marblehead lay just across the harbor. English had become involved in a lawsuit with William Beale over the ownership of some land there. Beale had been fuming over what he considered was the wrong the merchant had done him. Now he saw his chance to get even. He cried out upon English, and the girls in Salem Village, hearing of it, also cried out.

Philip English was willing enough to face the charge that he was a wizard. He was confident that both he and his wife would be cleared. But to surrender to the sheriff would hamper his efforts to get Mary transferred to Boston. He chose instead to go into hiding.

No one knows exactly where he went, but he had friends in high places in Boston who probably concealed him while he worked under cover in his wife's behalf. He was successful, and on May 13 she was brought from Salem Town to the prison in Boston. Then Philip resumed his efforts to get her released, but this he could not do. At last, on May 30, he surrendered himself.

At his examination in Salem Town, Susanna Sheldon was again the chief witness. The tale she told was familiar enough. Philip English and a "black man" had appeared to her. English told her the black man was her God and she must touch the book he held. When she refused, the merchant pinched her and threatened to kill her.

Although they were his fellow citizens of Salem Town and knew English well, the magistrates believed every word of Susanna's story and sent him to jail.

English was also able to have himself put in the prison in Boston, where he could be with Mary. The children were brought there and boarded with a Mrs. Holyitt.

There are varying accounts of what happened to the Englishes in prison. One has it that Philip English's friends were able to reach Governor Phips himself. It is said that Lady Mary Phips was a friend of Mary English and that she told her husband in no uncertain terms that he must do something about the two prisoners.

What is known is that they were treated much better than the other accused witches. Since he was a rich man, English may well have bribed guards to bring in food that was better than the moldy, wormy fare given other prisoners. And the Englishes do not seem to have been chained or put in one of the dreadful dungeons in the place.

It is known that they did have one special privilege. They were allowed to attend church. Each Sabbath, under guard, they were marched the short distance down Prison Lane and around the corner on Cornhill to the First Church.

Its pastor was the Reverend Joshua Moodey. Here was a Puritan minister who had ideas of his own about what was right and what was wrong, and had the courage to stand up for those beliefs.

Some years before, Mr. Moodey had been pastor of the church in Portsmouth, New Hampshire. The overbearing governor of the colony, Edward Cranfield, had tried to force the minister to use the service of the Church of England rather than the Puritan form. When Mr. Moodey refused, Cranfield sent word that he and some of his staff would come the following Sunday to receive from him "the sacrament of the Church of England."

Again Mr. Moodey refused to comply. Cranfield had him arrested and sent to prison for three months. When the minister was released, the First Church of Boston invited him to come there.

Mr. Moodey was even less pleased than Increase Mather with what was going on in regard to witchcraft. He was particularly incensed over the plight of the Englishes. Being a sensible man of high intelligence, he saw how ridiculous it was to believe these two could possibly be witches.

From the time Philip English arrived there, he and his wife spent about nine weeks in the prison. Then they were informed that a week from the following Monday they would be taken to Salem Town to stand trial before the Court of Oyer and Terminer.

On the following Sabbath they went as usual to the First Church. Mr. Moodey took his text that day from the Gospel according to St. Matthew: "But when they persecute you in this city, flee ye into another."

He looked straight at the Englishes as he read it. His sermon which followed was upon the wisdom of fleeing from injustice.

After the service, Mr. Moodey came to the prison to visit the Englishes, as he often did. "Did you take notice of my discourse?" he asked.

"Aye," said Philip English, "but I am not sure I understood it fully. Perhaps we should discuss it."

"The lives of both yourself and your wife are in danger," said the minister. "I strongly urge you to escape."

"I would rather face the judges of the court," replied English. "If I flee, I will stand convicted before it. All my property will be seized. I shall be a ruined man. Besides, we are both innocent. God will not suffer them to hurt us."

Mr. Moodey evidently believed in the famous advice

which Benjamin Franklin would express sixty-five years later: "God helps them that help themselves." He replied, "Many have suffered."

Mary English spoke up: "Do you think, Philip, that they who have suffered are innocent?"

"Aye," said her husband.

"Why, then, may we not suffer also? Take Mr. Moodey's advice, I pray you."

Philip English still hesitated. Then Mr. Moodey fixed him with his resolute gaze. "Philip," he said, "your wife's health has been impaired by her long stay in prison. She has a bad cough. If you do not take her away, I shall."

"Then I will do so if possible," English agreed.

"It can be done," said Moodey. "Leave it to me and your good friends in Boston."

Nothing happened during the week that followed. On the Sabbath, the day before they were to be taken to Salem Town for trial, the Englishes went to church as usual. When the service ended, the guards prepared to march them back to prison.

At the church door they were suddenly surrounded by a crowd of men milling about. As if by accident they jostled the guards back inside the church. The door slammed and its padlock snapped shut.

"Quick!" cried one of the men. "We have horses ready. Mount and ride as if the devil himself were after you. Head for New York, where you are expected."

In a trice, Philip and Mary English were off. Nothing had been neglected to aid their escape. One account has it that even the horses' shoes had been reversed to put pursuers off the track. Letters had been written to Governor Benjamin Fletcher of New York. When the Englishes' long journey to that province ended, he came out to greet them and showed them every courtesy.

In New York they were perfectly safe. There was not the fanatical belief in witches that existed in Massachusetts Bay and there had been no trouble with witchcraft.

The Englishes remained there until the witchcraft delusion was over. When they returned to Salem Town, their house was a shell. The sheriff had seized all of Philip English's property, furniture, livestock and seven of his ships. But such ill fortune did not daunt a man like Philip English. He was soon more prosperous than ever and once again one of Salem Town's most distinguished men.

As for the Reverend Joshua Moodey, the people of Boston were so enraged at what he had done that he was forced to leave. He returned to Portsmouth, where the troubles with the despotic Governor Cranfield were long past. Nor did the doughty Puritan minister regret what he had done. He had acted as his conscience told him to save two innocent people. With that he was content.

Another courageous couple were the Nathaniel Carys of Charlestown, just across the Charles River from Boston. Captain Cary had been a seafaring man and was now the prosperous owner of his own ships.

No one knows how Abigail Williams in Salem Village heard of the Carys or why she cried out on Mrs. Cary. Certainly she had never seen either of them. But word reached Charlestown that Abigail was talking about Elizabeth Cary.

The Carys were simple people who minded their own affairs and harmed no one. They could not understand it.

"We'll go to Salem Village and see what this is all about," said Captain Cary. He had no idea that it was the worst thing they could possibly have done.

Examinations of accused witches were being held the day they arrived. They went to the meetinghouse and managed to get seats where they could see and hear everything.

When the accused witches were brought in, the afflicted girls put on their usual show. The Carys were appalled. They had not expected anything so frightful.

At first the girls paid no attention to them. Then, noticing they were strangers to Salem Village, one came up and asked their names. They gave them, but this seemed to mean nothing to her.

When the morning session ended, the Carys went across the road to Deacon Ingersoll's tavern for some refreshment. John Indian, who sometimes worked there as a waiter, served them. Tituba's husband was quite a celebrity now and thoroughly enjoyed his notoriety.

"Sit down and have a mug of cider with us," said Captain Cary. "Tell us about the troubles in the village."

They would have done no worse to sit down with a rattlesnake. Over the cider, John Indian regaled them with tales of the plague of witches. Slipping off his shirt, he displayed some scars. "Look where the witches bit me," he boasted.

Captain Cary peered closely at them. He could see they were very old scars, but he said nothing.

Just then the afflicted girls were brought in. From the one who had spoken to the Carys in the meetinghouse, Abigail Williams had learned their names. They were all in full cry, like hounds after a hare.

"Cary! Cary!" they yelled.

A constable entered the tavern with a paper. He went up to Mrs. Cary. "I have a warrant from the magistrates for your arrest," he said.

They took her before Hathorne and Corwin that afternoon. "Stand with your arms outstretched," Hathorne ordered.

Mrs. Cary was in such a state of terror that she was on the verge of fainting. Her husband stepped forward to support her.

"Sit down," said Hathorne sternly. "She was strong enough to torment these children. She should be strong enough to stand."

Captain Cary was not used to such treatment. "You'll give me no orders!" he cried.

"Hold your tongue!" thundered Hathorne. "If you are not silent I'll have you removed."

Nevertheless, Nathaniel Cary remained standing by his wife. She was weeping hysterically, and he tenderly wiped away her tears and the beads of sweat on her forehead.

The girls were brought in. Leading them was the Carys' newfound "friend," John Indian. The slave fell writhing to the floor.

"Cary! Cary!" yelled the girls.

"Touch John Indian and relieve his agony," Hathorne told Mrs. Cary.

When she held out her hand, John Indian grabbed it and pulled her to the floor with him.

Instantly, Nathaniel Cary drew his rapier and lunged for him. Before he could run it through the slave, court attendants leaped forward and snatched the sword away.

"Elizabeth Cary," said Hathorne, "you are committed to Salem jail to await trial for witchcraft."

"God will take vengeance!" Captain Cary shouted. "God will deliver us from the hands of unmerciful men!"

To Hathorne he said, "I demand that you transfer my wife to the jail in Cambridge." Cambridge was in Middlesex County, and so was Charlestown then. Captain Cary was sure that if she were taken there he could use his influence to have her released.

His plea was refused, but later he was able to have her taken to the Cambridge jail. There his wealth and prominence enabled him to arrange an escape. There is no record of how this was accomplished, but probably he was able to bribe authorities and guards.

The Carys fled to Rhode Island, but they were pursued there and hastened on to New York. There, like the Englishes, they were safe.

One other prominent man was able to carry out his resolution not to submit to injustice. There was still a mysterious figure in the plague of witches who remained unknown—the "tall man of Boston" Tituba had mentioned in her testimony. The people of Salem Village gasped when they heard the afflicted girls had named him at last. "Can it be?" they whispered to one another.

So important was their discovery that William Stoughton himself ordered the man to report to Salem Village for examination. On May 28 he strode into the meetinghouse. Wearing his sword and keeping his hat on his head, he looked the girls up and down with contempt. He had never seen them before, nor had they seen him.

Everyone knew of Captain John Alden, just as they did of his famous father, John Alden, who had come to Plymouth in the *Mayflower* in 1620 and had married Priscilla Mullens. The younger John Alden had made a name for himself too. Like Sir William Phips, he had been both a sea captain and a soldier. In the bloody King Philip's War with the Indians he had distinguished himself for valor.

He certainly fitted Tituba's account of the man she had seen, for he was both tall and a resident of Boston. Of course, the description would have suited scores, even hundreds of other men, but it was John Alden the girls had picked out as their quarry.

The sight of him in the courtroom was enough to have put alarm into their hearts, however. Although he was now seventy years old, he was so muscular and ramrod-straight that he did not look his age. And he was in no mood for any nonsense.

There were those in the courtroom who knew he had cowed many a shirking sailor into trembling obedience with sea-dog's language that fairly smoked. Bartholomew Gedney, for one. Gedney, a member of the Court of Oyer and Terminer, which would sit in a few days, had joined the magistrates on the bench today in order to help his old friend John Alden. Even though Alden was confident he could clear himself of this ridiculous charge, he was glad to see Gedney there.

Alden took an inconspicuous seat among others in the courtroom. The girls made no outcry as he came in.

Hathorne spoke to them: "Point out the man from Boston who has hurt you."

The courtroom was as still as a graveyard at midnight while their bold eyes roved over it. A minute passed. The people were agog. Could it be that the girls were unable to recognize their tormentor?

At last one girl thrust out a skinny finger. "There he sits!" she shrieked. "There sits John Alden!"

The people were stunned. She was pointing at another man, a Captain Hill.

A spectator seated just behind the girl leaned over and whispered in her ear. Instantly she shifted her finger and aimed it at John Alden.

"Alden! Alden!" she cried.

"How do you know it is Alden?" Hathorne asked.

"The man told me."

The other girls set up a great hue and cry. One shrieked, "There sits Alden! A bold fellow, with his hat on before the judges! He sells powder to the Indians and French!"

The courtroom was in an uproar. Alden stood up, shouting to make himself heard: "There is not a word of truth in what she says!"

"He is nicking me with his sword!" howled one girl.

"He is pinching me!" charged another.

In a fury, Alden turned to the magistrates and said, "Just why do your honors suppose I have not better things to do than to come here and afflict these persons that I never knew or saw before?"

"Be silent!" admonished Hathorne. "Look upon these afflicted children."

As Alden did so, all the girls fell in a writhing heap at his feet.

He turned to the magistrates. He was looking straight at Bartholomew Gedney. "What's the reason *you* don't fall down when I look at you? Can you give me one?"

Gedney could not meet Alden's gaze. What he had just seen had changed his mind about helping his old friend. *Alden had knocked these girls down without even touching them.* Could there be any possible doubt of his guilt?

John Alden was committed to await trial. Nevertheless, the magistrates stood in enough awe of his high standing in the colony to let him remain, closely guarded, in his own home in Boston.

After what he had seen, John Alden was not fool enough to wait meekly for the Court of Oyer and Terminer to have its chance at him. He bribed one of his guards to look the other way before dawn one morning when he slipped away on a fast horse.

The next midnight there came a frantic hammering at the door of one of Alden's friends in Duxbury, near Plymouth, where he had lived before coming to Boston.

"Who's there?"

"John Alden! Let me in, for the devil himself is after me!"

In Duxbury his friends kept him hidden until the witchcraft delusion was over.

Meanwhile, in Salem Town, the Court of Oyer and Terminer had begun its sessions.

10

". . . To the Place of
Execution . . ."

On the morning of June 2, 1692, the courthouse on Town-House Lane in Salem Town was packed solid with those who had gotten there early enough to squeeze inside. On this, the first day of the witchcraft trials, Witch Bishop was to face the judges of the Court of Oyer and Terminer.

There were few if any who questioned Bridget Bishop's guilt. In fact, some of the latecomers massed along the way from the jail were given new proof of it. As Sheriff George Corwin and the prisoner passed the First Church of Salem Town, spectators within earshot were startled when an eerie clatter arose from the building.

They shuddered, looked at each other, and nodded their heads solemnly. Satan was surely at work . . .

It was windy that morning, but no one suggested the noise might be a flapping loose board of the old meetinghouse. Bridget Bishop's reputation was already too evil. There could be no doubt that the devil, enraged at the prospect of losing one of the creatures who did as he bade them, had caused the sound.

In the courtroom, the people waited expectantly. Before them, at the front of the room, sat the seven stony-faced judges, awesome in their black robes. There, in the jury box, were the twelve men who would decide Bridget Bishop's fate. The afflicted girls were there too, among other witnesses.

The spectators whispered to each other of the things they knew of Bridget Bishop.

"That tavern of hers on the Beverly road! Allowed young folks to loiter there at unseemly hours, she did, a-playing shovel-board! Disgraceful!"

"Aye, they say it went on as late as ten o'clock at night. Decent people roundabout couldn't sleep for the noise."

"What about her neighbor that claimed Bridget'd bewitched her? What was her name?"

"I forget. Five-six years ago, wa'n't it? Poor woman —found her stabbed to death with a pair of scissors. A witch's work, and plain enough who done it if ye ask *me*. They'd have hung Bridget then if they'd had a proper court like this one."

No one mentioned that the woman who had died was insane.

A muffled roar from the crowd outside the courthouse brought the people within bolt upright in their seats. All eyes were fixed on the courtroom door.

Bridget Bishop marched in defiantly. She wore what she had had on the day the magistrates had sent her to jail. The notorious tavernkeeper loved flashy clothes. Her gown was lavishly ornamented with laces and its bodice was bright red, an affront to Puritan Salem

Town. Now her finery was bedraggled and filthy; nevertheless, the sight inflamed the spectators.

It was like some grim, ghastly joke, this first witch trial. For the most part the judges were content to accept the evidence taken at Bridget's examination and written depositions signed by other accusers who simply swore to them in court. No friends appeared as witnesses in her behalf.

Nor did lawyers appear for the defense. There were few of them in Massachusetts Bay at that time, for they were in disrepute and were discouraged from appearing in any court. The cases against the accused witches were prepared by the colony's attorney general. But at the trial the judges were supreme, especially the merciless Chief Justice Stoughton.

The depositions were by neighbors and acquaintances of Goodwife Bishop. One man described how his little boy was taken with fits. He believed Bridget Bishop had bewitched him. Although he did not say why, the judges accepted his testimony.

Another man had awakened one morning in his bed-chamber to see Bridget Bishop standing there, grinning at him. Then, presto! she struck him on the head and flew through a tiny crevice in the window frame.

Others testified about strange occurrences they believed she had caused. Two men who had repaired the cellar wall of Bridget's house swore they found dolls of rags and hogs' bristles concealed there with pins stuck in them. Everyone knew a witch who made such a doll in the image of an enemy could cause that person's death by sticking pins into it.

One deposition was made by the Reverend John Hale of Beverly. He had examined the body of Christina Trask, the insane woman who claimed Bridget had bewitched her.

"As to the wounds she died of," he testified, "I observed three deadly ones. I then judged and still do apprehend it impossible for her with so short a pair of scissors to mangle herself without some extraordinary work of the devil or witchcraft."

He seemed to have forgotten he had said at the time that Goodwife Trask had committed suicide.

The jury soon returned with its decision: "We find Bridget Bishop guilty of all charges against her."

They brought her to stand before the judges.

"Bridget Bishop," said Stoughton, "you have been found guilty of the felonies and witchcrafts whereof you stood indicted. I accordingly direct that the high sheriff of Essex County, on Friday, the tenth of June, take you to the place of execution and that you be hanged by the neck until you are dead."

On that day Sheriff George Corwin took Bridget in a cart to Gallows Hill and hanged her.

There were many other accused witches in jail, but the court took a recess. Meanwhile, the judges conferred with a group of the most prominent ministers in the colony and asked for their advice on how the rest of the trials should be conducted.

The ministers were led by Increase Mather. He, of course, already had doubts. On June 15 he drew up a statement which all the others signed.

"We judge," one part of it said, "that in the prosecution of these and all such witchcrafts, there is need of a very critical and exquisite Caution, lest by too much Credulity for things received only upon the Devil's Authority, there be a Door opened for a long Train of miserable Consequences, and Satan get an advantage over us, for we should not be ignorant of his Devices."

Increase Mather was much concerned because the Court of Oyer and Terminer had accepted what was called "spectral evidence" in Bridget Bishop's trial. In the statement he said that such evidence, in which a person appeared as a "shape" of some sort and afflicted others, should not be considered. Much of the evidence against Bridget was of this very kind.

But with this caution, the ministers' statement concluded, "Nevertheless, We cannot but humbly recommend unto the Government, the speedy and vigorous Prosecution of such as have rendered themselves obnoxious, according to the Direction given in the Laws of God, and the wholesome Statutes of the English Nation, for the Detection of Witchcrafts."

It is not surprising that William Stoughton was not the one who asked that the conference be held. But the judge who did suggest it, John Richards, must have had some twinges of guilt over Bridget Bishop's trial. And soon another of the judges showed his feelings about it much more plainly.

Judge Saltonstall was a member of a distinguished Massachusetts Bay family which is still eminent today in the state of Massachusetts. A talented and fair-minded man, Nathaniel Saltonstall was sickened and revolted by what had passed for justice before the court. He declared he would sit no longer as one of its judges, and resigned.

He returned to his home in Haverhill, but he could not escape the memories of what he had seen and heard at the courthouse in Salem Town. He began to drink more than was good for him. Since he was still a member of the General Court, his friend Samuel Sewall saw him drunk there one day while it was in session and sent him a reproving letter.

"I was grieved," Sewall wrote, "when I heard and saw that you had drunk to excess; so that your head and hand were rendered less useful than at other times. Let me entreat you, Sir, to break off this practice."

What Samuel Sewall's own feelings were at this time, no one knows, for he made no mention of them in his famous diary. But he was able to continue sitting with the court when it resumed its sessions. As for Nathaniel Saltonstall's place, Governor Phips appointed in his stead Jonathan Corwin, the magistrate who had sat with John Hathorne during the examinations of the accused witches. Though he had not been as vindictive as Hathorne, Corwin was not bothered with Saltonstall's scruples.

The Court of Oyer and Terminer sat again on June 28. This time five accused witches were tried. There was Sarah Good, the frowsy hag Ann Putnam and Mercy Lewis had met on their way to the parsonage the day all the trouble had begun. Another was Susanna Martin of Amesbury, who had come so miraculously to call upon her treacherous friend in Newbury without getting her feet muddy. Elizabeth Howe of Ipswich and

Sarah Wildes of Topsfield, whose neighbors had cried out upon them, also faced the court. And there was feeble old Rebecca Nurse.

William Stoughton paid not the slightest attention to the ministers' statement. And as chief justice, his authority was not to be questioned. Almost all the evidence against the five women was of the "spectral" kind the ministers had warned against. Yet Stoughton let the witnesses tell their tales of the strange things the women's "shapes" had done.

When Sarah Good was tried, one of the afflicted girls screeched, "Goody Good attacked us with a knife!" From the pocket of her gown she drew a shiny bit of metal. "See! the knife broke off. Here is the piece."

This shocking evidence had the spectators sitting on the edges of their chairs. Surely here was proof that could not be denied.

Just then a young man stood up. His name has been lost, but his courage shines out.

"That's a piece of my knife," he said. "I broke it off yesterday while I was using it." He took out the knife. "Give me the broken piece."

Sullenly, the girl handed it over. The young man put it alongside his knife and held the two pieces up so that all could see. "It fits perfectly."

The girls glared at him, but none dared dispute his proof that their story was false.

It did not help Sarah Good. The testimony the girls had given at her examination was enough to condemn her, not to mention the tales villagers had told. The jury found her guilty and she was sentenced to die.

The judges wasted little time on the next three women. There were many charges against them by the girls and others. It made no difference that most of the evidence was "spectral." They were all condemned.

Rebecca Nurse's trial was quite another matter, however. There were a good many people who were not at all sure this decent, churchgoing woman and loving mother was a witch. She had her family and good friends who were not afraid to stand up for her.

She sat there in the courtroom with her head bowed. Although she scarcely seemed to know what was going on, her lips moved as if in prayer.

Mary Walcott and Abigail Williams swore that Rebecca had murdered several persons with the help of her sister, Sarah Cloyce. Ann Putnam's mother had also made a deposition charging that Rebecca's specter had boasted it had killed two men and one woman who had died some time before in Salem Village. Even Mr. Parris made a deposition telling of a case in which Rebecca's "shape" had caused a person to fall ill.

In spite of all this there was doubt on many a face in the courtroom. It showed in the jurymen's expressions. They were listening intently and they seemed uneasy.

There was nothing doubtful or merciful in William Stoughton's behavior, however. Once more he ignored the ministers' warning about spectral evidence in his charge to the jury. Indeed, if he had warned them not to consider it there would have been nothing on which to convict Rebecca Nurse.

The jury retired to the nearby house of Jonathan

Corwin, the magistrate. They spent a long time in considering their verdict. When at last they returned there was a breathless silence in the courtroom.

The foreman, Thomas Fisk, spoke: "We find the defendant, Rebecca Nurse, not guilty of the charges against her."

The courtroom could not have been in greater tumult if a powder keg had exploded there. Stoughton tried vainly to restore order. One of the judges, as he rose to leave, managed to make himself heard above the uproar.

"I will have this witch indicted again!" he shouted.

Stoughton motioned him to remain. Then the chief justice addressed the jury: "I will not impose upon you, but I must ask if you have considered one statement made by the prisoner. When Deliverance Hobbs was brought into court to testify, the prisoner turned her head to her and said, 'What, do you bring her? She is one of us.' Has the jury weighed the implications of this statement?"

Deliverance Hobbs was one of the accused women awaiting trial. At her examination she had confessed to being a witch. What Stoughton meant was that by saying, "She is one of us," Rebecca was admitting that she too was a witch.

Thomas Fisk hesitated, scratching his head. "I can't remember, Your Honor," he said finally. "We will retire again and consider it."

After some time Fisk returned to the courtroom. "The others have sent me back to ask the prisoner what she meant," he said.

He approached Rebecca and stood before her. "You said the witness Deliverance Hobbs was one of you. What did it mean, Goodwife Nurse?"

Rebecca seemed to be in a trance. She looked at Fisk, but her eyes were glazed as if she did not see him. She made no reply.

Fisk rejoined the other jurors. Soon they returned to the courtroom. They found Rebecca Nurse guilty of witchcraft. Then the ruthless Stoughton sentenced her to death.

Rebecca collapsed and had to be carried back to the jail. But the Puritan witch hunters were not yet through with her. On the following Sabbath she was carried to the meetinghouse in Salem Town, where they sat her down in a chair at the head of the broad aisle. The congregation that day filled every seat on the main floor and gallery, with some people perched precariously on the windows.

Then the Reverend Nicholas Noyes read the solemn words excommunicating Rebecca from the Puritan church. It meant that she was being handed over to Satan and doomed to eternal hellfire.

It did not keep Rebecca's loyal family from standing by her in this desperate hour. Some of her sons and sons-in-law went to her in the jail.

"Thomas Fisk stood before you in the courtroom and asked you a question, Mother," one son shouted in her ear. "Why didn't you answer?"

"I remember naught of it!" she cried. "I did not see him there."

"He asked why you spoke of Deliverance Hobbs as 'one of us' when she came into court. Why did you, mother?"

"I meant that Goody Hobbs was a prisoner like the rest of us."

There was no time to be lost. These men of Rebecca's family set out at once for Boston. They took with them a petition signed by twenty-two respectable citizens of Salem Village, certifying to her blameless character and their belief that she was no witch. They also had Rebecca's explanation, in writing, of why she had spoken of the confessed witch, Deliverance Hobbs, as "one of us."

Governor Phips was busy preparing for his expedition to Maine, but the men of the Nurse family were persistent. At last Phips granted them an interview.

There can be little doubt that Increase Mather had heard about Stoughton's conduct at the second session of the court, and was greatly disturbed. No doubt, too, the governor had talked with his friend and benefactor about it. He signed an order reprieving Rebecca Nurse from the gallows until an investigation could be made.

But within a few days word reached Phips that news of the reprieve had caused a catastrophe in Salem Village. Devils were tormenting the afflicted girls so sorely that some of them were dying.

Perhaps this was the time for Sir William Phips to have stood firm against the witch hunters. Yet this was the very crest of the wave of fear and hatred of witches that was sweeping Massachusetts Bay. Probably the governor was told that a menacing rabble had surged about the courthouse while Rebecca Nurse was being tried, howling for her doom. If some of the girls died, it might set off a rebellion worse than the one which had deposed Governor Andros. Phips cancelled the reprieve.

The five miserable women tried and convicted of witchcraft at the second session of the Court of Oyer and Terminer were the ones who were taken to Gallows Hill and hanged on July 19.

11

Wizards Too

The Court of Oyer and Terminer did not sit again until August 5. That was the day after Sir William Phips sailed with his expedition to the coast of Maine. It was almost as though Stoughton and the other judges felt safer with the governor away before going on with their dreadful work.

Phips had assembled a strong force of 450 soldiers, with six ships to carry them to the ruined fort at Pemaquid. He also took with him Major Benjamin Church of the Rhode Island colony. Here was a name to strike terror into the heart of every Indian in New England.

In 1675 the powerful sachem of the Wampanoags, King Philip, united all the Indian tribes of Massachusetts Bay, the then separate colony of Plymouth, and Rhode Island in an effort to drive out all the settlers of those regions. A colonial army was sent against them, but its commander did not know how to fight in the stealthy fashion of the savages. King Philip's warriors swooped down on isolated villages, tomahawking the people and burning their houses.

Benjamin Church understood how to meet the Indians in their own way. He organized a band of rangers. They were woodsmen like himself, crack shots, and able to move swiftly and noiselessly through the swamps and dense forests. Church and his men finally tracked King Philip down in a vast swamp in Rhode Island and shot him dead, ending the war.

Although the Abenakis and Micmacs of Maine and Canada had not taken part in King Philip's War, they had heard of Benjamin Church's deeds. When Phips' expedition landed at Pemaquid, the news spread quickly through the wilderness that Church had come. There were no more raids on isolated settlements of the region. The Indians from Canada slunk home, and those who lived in Maine lay low.

Phips sent Church farther east with a detachment of woodsmen to scout for Indians. Then he and the rest of his men set to rebuilding the fort. The ships had brought cannon, shot, powder and other equipment and materials needed.

Phips enjoyed himself hugely. This was the sort of thing he was best at—action, leading men under his command. He was sure that once the fort was rebuilt there would be no more trouble with French and Indian raids in Maine.

He was sure too that when he returned to Massachusetts Bay the people would be grateful. If the French and Indians were able to destroy all the Maine settlements it would not be long before they ventured into the villages surrounding Boston. The French objective in this first of the colonial wars, King William's, was to drive all English settlers from America. The fort at

Pemaquid would be a bulwark to save the Bay Colony, including Boston.

Probably Phips was also glad to be far from where the plague of witches was raging. If his conscience pricked him for going off in the midst of it, he was too busy to let it bother him much. He could tell himself that he had taken the proper measures against witchcraft. The Court of Oyer and Terminer was surely in good hands under able Lieutenant Governor Stoughton.

Meanwhile, in Salem Town, the court held its third session. Six persons were tried—George Burroughs, John Procter and his wife Elizabeth, George Jacobs, Sr., John Willard and Martha Carrier.

There was plenty of excitement for the spectators in all these trials, but the most dramatic was that of the "little black minister" of Casco Bay, Mr. Burroughs. People were still stunned to think that a clergyman could have sold out to the devil.

Mr. Burroughs was a simple man and ordinarily a mild one, but now that he had recovered from his first shock and bewilderment, he was indignant. He had prepared an appeal to the jury, which he read in court. In it he denied there was any such thing as witchcraft.

"There neither are nor ever were witches that, having made a contract with the devil, can send a devil to torment other people at a distance," he had written.

Such a brazen statement would probably have been enough to convict him even if there had been no other evidence, but there was—a great deal of it.

Two witnesses from Casco Bay had made depositions about incredible feats of strength performed by the minister which could only have been done with the aid of Satan. Burroughs was a small man, and to the spectators it seemed that the devil must surely have been mixed up in such deeds. But his size was deceiving. He was immensely powerful, with arm and leg muscles like spring steel. He admitted he had done these things, but without supernatural aid.

The worst evidence against him was that which several of the afflicted girls had given at his examination, especially Ann Putnam's testimony that his specter had boasted to her of three murders. And while the trial was going on, one of the girls spoke out: "Last night he sent his shape to bite us." She held out her arm. "Look! There are the tooth marks!"

The judges examined her arm. "Have the prisoner's mouth pried open," Chief Justice Stoughton ordered.

When this had been done, the judges peered at Burroughs' teeth, then at the marks on the girl's arm. They nodded their heads. The marks of George Burroughs' teeth, beyond any doubt, they agreed. After that, the "little black minister" had no chance of escaping the gallows. He was sentenced to die.

When the Procters faced the court, a petition signed by fifty-two of their friends and neighbors was presented. It declared they could not possibly be witches. And toothless old George Jacobs' granddaughter Margaret tried to save him. Hateful neighbors who had cried out on him tricked Margaret into confessing that she was a witch and her grandfather a wizard. Later she made a deposition denying everything she had said.

No one tried to help John Willard or Martha Carrier.

As a deputy constable, Willard had arrested some of the accused witches. Then he decided something was wrong about it and said so. He fled when the afflicted girls cried out on him, but he was captured. As for the sharp-tongued Martha, spiteful neighbors had had her seized. They frightened her seven-year-old daughter into testifying that her mother was a witch.

The efforts to help the Procters and George Jacobs came to nothing. All six of the persons who were tried at the third session of the court were condemned.

Elizabeth Procter was not to die with her husband, however. Stoughton reprieved her until the baby she was expecting could be born. Harsh as Puritan justice was, it would not send an innocent unborn child to its death. Later, the sheriff could take Goodwife Procter to Gallows Hill.

What happened there on August 19 when the other five were hanged was told by a mysterious man, Robert Calef of Boston. Little is known of him except that he was a merchant and an enemy of the Mathers. Strangely, he believed in witches, but he was outraged at the injustice of the trials in Salem Town.

As George Burroughs stood on the ladder that day with the noose about his neck, Calef wrote, he spoke to the crowd assembled to see him die. His words, as he proclaimed his innocence, were simple, but they had a profound effect on the spectators, especially when he concluded by reciting the Lord's Prayer.

A muttering of protest arose among the watchers, increasing rapidly in volume. No one urged them or gave an order, but as if by a resolution common to all of them they surged forward toward the ladder.

"Save him!" came a shout. "Take the rope off his neck!"

Another man cried, "No wizard could repeat the Lord's Prayer at a time like this. God would not have it!"

Was George Burroughs to be saved? He might well have been, but for an authoritative voice among the crowd: "Stay! Let me be heard!"

They turned to see who had spoken. They saw a young man all in black, mounted on a horse. He had raised himself in his stirrups so he could better be seen. It was Cotton Mather.

"Let me remind you," said Mather, "that the devil is never more himself than when he appears to be an angel of light. This man is not what he appears to be."

Among those who had resolved to save George Burroughs, not one dared to dispute the eminent minister. Now they let the sheriff hang the "little black minister" of Casco Bay.

Some historians do not believe this tale of Robert Calef's. Yet under the date of August 19, 1692, Samuel Sewall wrote in his diary: "George Burroughs, John Willard, Jno. Procter, Martha Carrier and George Jacobs were executed at Salem, a very great mob of spectators being present. Mr. Cotton Mather was there . . ." And he added, "Mr. Burroughs by his Speech, Prayer, protestation of his Innocence, did much move unthinking persons, which occasions their speaking hardly concerning his being executed."

The Court of Oyer and Terminer recessed until September 9. Then it sat, tried six accused witches, and condemned them. Eight days later, on September 17, it met again to try and convict nine more.

Something was different about these two sessions. Of the fifteen persons convicted and sentenced, only eight were hanged.

Abigail Faulkner, one of the seven who were not executed, was the daughter of the minister in Amesbury. Like Elizabeth Procter, she was expecting a baby and was given a reprieve. Another woman, Mary Bradbury of Salisbury, escaped. Some of her friends managed to slip her out of jail and away to concealment and safety.

A curious thing about the other five who never reached Gallows Hill was that all of them had confessed they were witches. Indeed, out of all the hundreds of persons jailed during the witchcraft delusion, not a single one who confessed to being a witch was executed. Many were never tried. Only the stouthearted ones who refused to confess something of which they were innocent were hanged.

The reason seems to be that the magistrates who conducted the examinations wanted the confessed witches kept alive, believing they would point out others. A good many did do so.

Some of those who confessed, like Tituba and Abigail Hobbs, did so at once, aware that it was a good way to save their skins. Others persisted in maintaining their innocence until the very shadow of the gallows fell upon them.

The seven women and one man who did not confess and were convicted were hanged on September 22. They included Rebecca Nurse's saintly sister, Mary Esty.

One other person was brought before the court at the session of September 17. He was Giles Cory, whose wife Martha was tried and condemned September 9 and hanged September 22.

The fearless Giles had made up his mind that he would not stand trial for a crime he had not commited. Once his decision was made, not even a frightful death budged him from it.

When they brought him into court and asked how he pleaded to the charge against him, he set his jaw and answered never a word. They coaxed and threatened him in vain.

What was to be done? The law required that a prisoner must make a plea. How could Giles be tried without one?

Someone, probably one of the judges well versed in English law, remembered what had been done in Europe in centuries past in such cases. A person who "stood mute," as the expression was, could be subjected to *peine forte et dure.*

The words are French, and they mean "painful and merciless punishment." This sentence for standing mute was that the prisoner be laid on his back while as great a weight as he could bear was placed on his body.

Giles Cory was taken from the jail in Salem Town to a vacant lot nearby. They laid him flat on the ground and piled heavy stones on his chest, one by one. Each time Giles groaned, but said nothing. They piled on more weight.

Probably they did not intend to kill him, for *peine forte et dure* was not supposed to be a means of execution. Doubtless they thought the agony would force a plea of innocent or guilty from him, so that he could be tried.

Iron-willed Giles Cory spoke not a word, however. And at last he died.

12

"This Court Must Fall!"

Winter comes early to Maine, and the winds of autumn were chill with the promise of colder weather when the fort at Pemaquid was finished. It stood near the shore, a grim warning to the keen-eyed Indian scouts who had watched its construction from the cover of the forest. Most of the savages had left the region. Benjamin Church and his detachment, roving the wilderness, had discovered only one Abenaki village. They had destroyed it, killing all the warriors who were unable to flee in time.

Sir William Phips was proud of what he had accomplished. He detailed ninety men to remain at the fort as a garrison, ready to move swiftly in pursuit of raiders if there were any more attacks on the settlements. And with that, he and the rest of his men sailed for Boston.

When he reached his home in the Green Lane, he found Lady Phips even more agitated than when he had returned from England.

"The witchcraft troubles are a disgrace to this colony!" she declared. "You must do something, William!"

"How is this?" asked her husband. "Does not the Court of Oyer and Terminer give the accused persons a speedy trial?"

"How can it?" she demanded. "The jails are filled to bursting with miserable people. More are being arrested each day."

"But the court had already held two sessions before I went away. Has it done naught since then?"

"Naught!" cried his wife. "It has condemned twenty-six persons, and nineteen have been hanged. One poor man has been pressed to death. The others await execution. I am sure there were some innocent ones among those who died. And many others, I am certain, still languish in jail—save one wretched woman. I am glad to say *she* has been freed."

"Freed? Who released her?"

"I did," replied Lady Phips calmly.

"*What?*" Phips roared. "By what authority did you do this?"

"Mine," said his wife. "The poor creature managed to have a note smuggled to me, protesting her innocence. I went to see her in that cold, foul prison. After talking with her, I was convinced she was no witch. Since you were far away and could not issue a warrant for her release, *I* signed one."

"They let her out?" Phips gasped.

"Of course. They dared not refuse the governor's wife. Do you know what people are saying of me?" Lady Phips smiled proudly. "They are calling me the pluckiest woman in Boston. But I am sure there are many other cases equally deserving. I want you to act, William."

"I will look into this," Phips promised. "But I think

you are unduly distraught, my dear. The judges of the Court of Oyer and Terminer are persons of the best prudence and figure I could pitch upon. They are better able than you to determine who is a witch and who not."

"William," said Mary Phips, "what would you think if *I* were accused as a witch?"

Phips laughed. "Ridiculous! But that will never happen, you may be sure."

"Do you think so?" asked his wife sweetly. "Then it will surprise you to know that the afflicted girls of Salem Village, hearing that I released that poor woman from prison, have cried out on me. You have returned just in time to save me from being arrested."

Phips charged out of his house to the stables, where he ordered his fine horse saddled. Then he galloped forth into the town.

First he went to the Town House, hoping to find his Council in session there. The Council Chamber was deserted. Then he cantered back to the North End and to William Stoughton's splendid mansion there.

Just what the governor said to the chief justice behind closed doors has never been revealed. It is known, however, that Stoughton expressed his unyielding opposition to any action which would weaken the authority of the Court of Oyer and Terminer.

When Phips left he rode straight to the prison. There he summoned John Arnold, the jailer, and was conducted on an inspection of the crowded place. He found the prisoners ragged, shivering in the cold, ill fed and and in despair.

Next, Phips returned to the Town House. Word that he had been there earlier had spread, and he found the members of his Council awaiting him.

Phips told them what he had seen and heard. "This court must fall!" he thundered.

Then he summoned an aide. "Fetch me the mittimuses for all those in prison awaiting trial for witchcraft."

These were the warrants under which the accused witches had been arrested. When the governor had them before him, he studied each one with care. In this he would have had the help of trained legal minds among his Council, because of his own small knowledge of the law.

About fifty of the warrants were found to have legal flaws in the way they were drawn up. This was the loophole Phips had been seeking.

Although a good many thinking persons now seriously questioned what had been done, the mass of the people still believed that those who had been executed were indeed witches. They were sure too that many more remained unpunished. And in spite of their solemn warning to the Court of Oyer and Terminer, most of the Puritan ministers still favored continuing the trials until every witch was exposed and destroyed.

Phips faced an aroused public opinion if he put an abrupt end to the trials. But since these fifty warrants were legally defective, he was justified in acting on them.

"Release these prisoners on bail," he ordered. Then he discharged the jailer in the Boston prison. A new one was appointed with instructions to see that the sufferings of the remaining prisoners were relieved.

Many people applauded the governor's action, but there was also much muttering against him.

On October 29, 1692, Phips issued an order dismissing the Court of Oyer and Terminer. But there remained the problem of what to do about the other accused witches still in jail. Under the law they must be tried. The records indicate that about 150 were imprisoned at that time.

Phips appointed five judges to a Superior Court of Adjudicature. Except for Thomas Danforth, all had sat on the Court of Oyer and Terminer. But most of them seem to have been the more tolerant ones.

Among them was John Richards, who had showed his doubts about the court's actions by asking that the Boston ministers be consulted. Samuel Sewall too, in view of what happened later, must sometimes have doubted. And while Thomas Danforth had shown himself stern enough when he presided over the examinations held in Salem Town, he had been a strong advocate of men's liberties in his seventy years. Probably he took up his duties with a new and more lenient view of how the new court should act.

Unfortunately, the chief justice of the new court was William Stoughton. Phips cannot be wholly blamed for Stoughton's reappointment, since the judges were chosen by a vote of the governor and the members of his Council. Doubtless Sir William could have been chosen himself if he had wished, but again his ignorance of the law scarcely fitted him for it.

Phips must have striven to impress upon all that the accused witches must be given completely fair trials. In Stoughton's case, some might have compared this to telling a hungry cannibal not to eat a missionary.

Of course, Lady Phips was never arrested as a witch. In one way or another the mouths of the afflicted girls in Salem Village were hushed up.

This was not the first time they had gone too far. They had cried out on the Reverend Samuel Willard of the Third Church in Boston. Willard was a minister as forthright as Joshua Moodey. He did not like what was going on in the witchcraft trials and spoke his mind about it. He was too important a figure to be arrested, however. The girls were told they had confused him with the former constable of Groton, John Willard, who was executed.

Nor would these incidents be the last of the girls' reckless charges. And in time they had their effect in making people realize that wrong was being done.

One man discovered a way no one else had thought of to shut his accusers up. He is identified in the records only as a "gentleman from Boston." He went to court and got a writ for the arrest of those who had charged him, bringing a suit for defaming his character and asking £1000 damages. He announced he would have it served if he heard any more about his being a wizard. He heard no more.

Meanwhile, among the Boston ministers, even Cotton Mather was beginning to question what was happening. He wrote a pamphlet called *Cases of Conscience Concerning Evil Spirits Personating Men*. The fourteen ministers who had given the warning to the Court of Oyer and Terminer showed their approval of the treatise by signing it.

In it Mather said, "If a Crime cannot be found out but by Miracle, it is not for any Judge on Earth to usurp that Judgment which is reserved for the Divine Throne." Yet at the same time he told of being present at George Burroughs' trial, and commented, "Had I been one of his Judges, I could not have acquitted him."

Having acted in the witchcraft delusion, Governor Phips decided he had better let the King and Queen know what he had done. He wrote a report to them, which Queen Mary later acknowledged with a letter commending him.

As yet, however, the doubts of the Boston ministers and other prominent persons did nothing to stop or even abate the witchcraft delusion. By now it had spread through a wide circle of villages in the countryside surrounding Boston—Billerica, Lynn, Boxford, Rowley, Marblehead, Gloucester, Woburn, Reading, Malden and others—as well as Boston itself.

Indeed, Satan's diabolical mischief-making was no longer centered in Salem Village. It was at its worst in Andover, nearly twenty miles away. For weeks, decent citizens of that village lived in dread, never sure that tomorrow would not find them in jail.

It began when the wife of an Andover man, Joseph Ballard, fell ill. The medicine the doctor dosed her with did her no good. Goodman Ballard was much troubled. On sober reflection he wondered . . . could it be that her affliction was of an unearthly kind . . . ?

He saddled a horse and rode to Salem Village. When he returned to Andover, Ann Putnam and Mary Walcott came with him.

The visit of two such famous characters to Andover caused a sensation. In no time a crowd collected before Joseph Ballard's house while Ann and Mary were in Goodwife Ballard's bedchamber.

The two girls charged that she was bewitched. When they came outside there were cries from the crowd in the dooryard.

"Come to my house! My husband is sick!"

"My mother is afflicted. I vow she's bewitched. Pray come and view her."

The girls were glad to oblige. They visited a score of houses where people lay ill. In every one they found that witchcraft was at work.

Then they began to name witches. They must have known few, if any, people in Andover; true, they had cried out on Martha Carrier there, but only after her neighbors had accused her. However, there were many residents of the village who were glad to pay off old scores by telling tales of strange doings by neighbors they did not like.

In the town hall the girls and other accusers made their charges before the village magistrate, Dudley Bradstreet. He was one of old Governor Simon Bradstreet's sons, and like his father a good and kindly man. He was shocked at what was going on, but he had his duty to perform. The truth must be discovered about the accused witches.

Bradstreet must have had writer's cramp after signing

forty warrants for the arrest of the accused persons. But it was not that which caused him to put a halt to the proceedings. His good sense told him it was ridiculous that so many people in the little village could all be witches.

The accusers were not through with their crying out, but Bradstreet held up his hand.

"I will sign no more warrants," he declared firmly.

The throng before him glared angrily. "Why not?" came a snarl. "There are others who are afflicting our people."

"I refuse on the ground that the evidence against them is not sufficient," said Bradstreet. And he left the town hall.

Ann Putnam and Mary Walcott were outraged. "He is a wizard!" they both cried.

At first this was a little too much for most people to swallow. Dudley Bradstreet was the foremost citizen of Andover and its representative in the General Court. Yet they wondered . . . the afflicted girls of Salem Village had discovered many a witch. Why should they be wrong about Dudley Bradstreet?

The girls did not stop with crying out on Bradstreet. "His wife is a witch!" they now charged.

Bradstreet had been determined to fight the charge against himself, but when his wife was accused he remembered what had happened to Elizabeth Procter because her husband had tried to stop his afflicted servant girl's mouth. Elizabeth was awaiting execution, once her child was born.

"Pack up your things," he told Mrs. Bradstreet. "We must leave Andover at once."

"But where will we go, Dudley?" she cried.

"To the Piscataqua," he replied. "We will be safe there."

In the darkness that night, the Bradstreets rode out of Andover, heading north. They did not stop until they were over the border between Massachusetts Bay and the New Hampshire province. In Portsmouth, at the mouth of the Piscataqua River, they remained until the witchcraft delusion was over.

Since the afflicted girls had been cheated of their revenge, they took it out upon one of their neighbors in Salem Village. He was John Bradstreet, another of the aged governor's sons. They charged him with having bewitched a dog. He too fled to New Hampshire.

In Andover, the witch hunt went on, with the village constables, hauling accused witches off to jail in Salem Town.

Another forthright minister of Massachusetts Bay was the Reverend Francis Dane of the church in Andover. He was appalled at the terror which had the village in its grip. The good old man heard some strange tales from members of his own congregation who claimed they had been bewitched by others.

One of them, William Barker, confessed, "I signed the devil's book. Satan promised he would pay all my debts and see that I lived comfortably all the rest of my days."

"I do not believe you, William," said Mr. Dane sternly.

Some women of his flock came to see him. "We flew through the air at midnight to Five Mile Pond," one said. "The devil baptized us there."

"You have been having bad dreams," said the minister.

He decided something must be done to end the senseless witch hunt, and he told others so. Some malevolent people in Andover wanted to see him arrested. They talked to an old woman, Ann Foster, who had been jailed after admitting she was a witch.

"I rode to Salem Village with Martha Carrier on a broomstick one night," she told them. "There were five hundred witches gathered there. One looked like Mr. Dane."

Even with this evidence, no one was brave enough to accuse the minister. But the afflicted girls took out their rage upon his family.

First they cried out on Abigail Faulkner, one of his married daughters. It has already been told how she was convicted but reprieved because she was expecting a baby. Some of the witch hunters went to work on two of her small daughters, Dorothy, who was ten, and Abigail, eight. At their mother's examination the two little girls said she had turned them into witches.

Then the afflicted ones turned on another of Mr. Dane's daughters, Elizabeth Johnson. One of her children, Elizabeth, was brought to the examination. The girl became so terrified that she said she too was a witch, had tormented many persons and had been baptized in a well by the devil. Goodwife Johnson too was sent to prison.

Where would the plague of witches strike next? It
seemed there was nothing to prevent its falling upon
other villages with the same devastating effect. Yet the
lines written by the Greek poet Euripides around 414
B.C.—

> *How oft the darkest hour of ill*
> *Breaks brightest into dawn*

—were as true in the seventeenth century as they were
then and are today. A change was coming.

13

The End of It

The Superior Court of Adjudicature met for its first session in Salem Town on January 3, 1693. By that time the tide of the witch hunt had passed its flood and was ebbing swiftly.

There were scores of angry people now. In Andover, seven men sent a petition to Governor Phips demanding the release on bail of their wives, in Salem Town jail accused of witchcraft, as well as their children, who were there with their mothers.

Two weeks later, twenty-four citizens of Andover drew up a statement in which they called the afflicted girls of Salem Village "distempered persons." "Distempered" is an old New England word meaning "sick."

Increase Mather was becoming more and more impatient with the way things were going. A member of his congregation had taken his sick child to Salem Village so that the afflicted girls could tell whether it was bewitched.

"Is there not a God in Boston that you should go to the devil in Salem?" the minister snapped irritably.

Thomas Brattle was one of the richest merchants in

Boston, and a benefactor who gave large sums of money to Harvard College and for public projects. He was seriously disturbed over the witchcraft troubles and made a thorough investigation of them. When a minister, whose name is unknown, asked for Mr. Brattle's advice as to what should be done, he wrote a pamphlet which he called *Account of Witchcraft in the County of Essex, 1692.*

Mr. Brattle minced no words in giving his opinion of the examinations and trials. He called them "rude and barbarous methods." Of the witchcraft delusion, he added, "I think it deserves the name of Salem superstition and sorcery, and it is not fit to be named in a land of such light as New England is."

He had some comments about the witnesses. "They are deluded, imposed upon, and under the influence of some evil spirit," he wrote, "and therefore unfit to be evidences either against themselves or anyone else." He said it was disgraceful that the magistrates would accept evidence based on common gossip, irresponsible confessions and the claims of the afflicted girls. As for the girls themselves, he called them liars and mountebanks.

Mr. Brattle spoke of the rising indignation in the colony. "There are several about the Bay," he wrote, "men of understanding, judgment and piety . . . that do utterly condemn the said proceedings, and do freely deliver their judgment in the case to be this, viz: that these methods will utterly undo poor New England." Among them he named Simon Bradstreet, Thomas Danforth, Increase Mather, Samuel Willard and Nathaniel Saltonstall.

He did not think so well of the ministers of Beverly, Salem Town and Salem Village—John Hale, Nicholas Noyes and Samuel Parris. But except for them, he said, "the reverend elders throughout the country are very much dissatisfied." And he added, "The principal men of Boston, and thereabout, are generally agreed that irregular and dangerous methods have been taken as to these matters."

As if to make up for its delay in getting started, the Superior Court of Adjudicature tried fifty-two accused witches at its sessions which began January 3 and lasted until May. This time the ruthless William Stoughton could not prevail against aroused public opinion.

Moreover, the other judges were much more tolerant now. Courageous Samuel Willard, the minister, strove to impress upon three who were members of his congregation that the prisoners must have fair trials. They were able to see to it that no "spectral evidence" was accepted by the new court.

Nevertheless, Stoughton tried to conduct this court as he had the old one. But his efforts did not sway the jurymen. Without "spectral evidence" there was little enough to prove a person's guilt. The jurors found all but three of the fifty-two innocent.

In a rage, Stoughton sentenced the three to death. He issued warrants for their speedy execution, as well as for the five confessed witches who had so far escaped the gallows although they had been condemned.

Sir William Phips then summoned the chief justice before him. The governor had reached a decision.

"There will be no more trials," he said. "I am dis-

charging all the rest of those who are in prison accused
of witchcraft. I am also issuing a proclamation of pardon
for all of them, including those you have sentenced to
death. It will include those who fled from the injustice
of the Court of Oyer and Terminer."

Stoughton's face, usually so pale and cold, was suf-
fused with fury. He fairly exploded in a denunciation
of all those who had interfered with his efforts to destroy every accused witch.

"We were in a way to have cleared the land of
them!" he shouted. "Who it is that obstructs the cause
of justice, I know not. The Lord be merciful to the
country!" And he stormed out of the room.

The doors of the jails then swung open for a host of
miserable people. The records indicate that about 150
were freed. Thomas Hutchinson, who was the last royal
governor of Massachusetts Bay before the American
Revolution, wrote a history of the province which is
considered an authority on its colonial times. In it,
speaking of Phips' proclamation, he wrote, "Such a jail
delivery has never been known in New England."

Unfortunately, Sir William's action did not mean
that the sufferings of all the prisoners were ended. The
law required that before they could be released, all the
costs connected with their arrest and imprisonment
must be paid.

This was all very well for those who had the money
to pay, or whose relatives and friends could raise it. But
some were poor farming people who had all they could
do to make a living and had no one to help them finan-

cially. Some remained in jail many weeks until the money could somehow be obtained.

Several of these wretched prisoners died in jail. One, Sarah Daston, had been acquitted by the new court, but had no money to pay for her freedom. Another was the confessed witch, Ann Foster, who had tried to implicate Mr. Dane, the Andover minister, as a wizard. Sarah Osburne, who had been condemned, had already died in Boston Prison on March 10, 1693.

Those who had escaped from prison or had fled before they could be jailed now returned to their homes under Phips' proclamation of pardon—the Englishes, Carys, the two sons of Governor Bradstreet, and others.

John Alden was already back. In the latter part of April it was plain that he had no more to fear, and he resolved to stand trial. On April 30, 1693, he strode glowering before the Superior Court of Adjudicature in Boston. No one appeared as a witness against him, and he was discharged for lack of evidence.

The terrible witchcraft delusion was over. Yet in a sense it was not, nor would it be for many a year. Its effects still lingered, causing strife, bitterness, heartache and shame—especially shame. What happened during those years that followed Sir William Phips' proclamation of pardon remains to be told.

14

Guilt

What happened in Salem Village had torn it asunder almost as surely as if a tornado had ripped and whirled through it.

It was split into two factions. On one side were those who had survived the terrible ordeal of arrest and imprisonment, their families, and the families of the men and women who had been executed. On the other were the people who had caused all this misery. A few months before, they had been the accusers, but now they were the accused.

As usual, when some great injustice is brought to light, no one wanted to take the blame. The guilty ones set about to find a scapegoat, thinking this would ease their own consciences.

Who but the Reverend Samuel Parris had caused this dishonor to fall upon Salem Village? The witchcraft delusion had begun right in his house. He had ferreted out the afflicted girls' secret of their sessions with Tituba. And he had relentlessly pursued his hunt for the witches he believed had tormented them. The congregation decided to drive him out.

In April, 1693, they passed a resolution stopping payment of Mr. Parris' salary. He was not one to submit tamely, however. He started a lawsuit, demanding payment.

The congregation struck back with a petition to the court. "Mr. Parris," it said, "has been the beginner and procurer of the sorest affliction, not to the village only, but to the whole country."

The lawsuit dragged on for several years, but this did not change the congregation's determination to be rid of its minister. Its leaders included not only those with guilty consciences, but the ones who had suffered most, especially the members of poor Rebecca Nurse's family. And most of Salem Village supported them.

Mr. Parris was hounded as he had hounded accused witches, but he hung on doggedly. At last he made one concession. He stood before his flock one Sabbath and read a kind of confession to them. It was called *Meditations of Peace.*

He admitted that the devil might take on the shape of persons who were innocent of any connection with him. "I beg, entreat and beseech you," he had written, "that Satan, the devil, the roaring lion, the old dragon, the enemy of all righteousness may no longer be served by us."

Then the minister offered his sympathy "to those who have suffered through the clouds of human weakness and Satan's wiles and sophistry." In a prayer he asked that God forgive him, and that all his flock "be covered with the mantle of love and we may forgive each other heartily, sincerely and thoroughly."

Whether the relatives and friends of those who had been hanged were comforted by his sympathy is not known, but they did not forgive him heartily. They went right on trying to drive him out.

At last, in 1695, the ministers of the villages north of Boston held a meeting in Salem Town to discuss what could be done to end the dispute. Mr. Parris finally agreed to go if his congregation would pay him £79, 9 shillings, sixpence he claimed they owed him. They decided it was well worth that sum to be rid of him. Then he and his family left Salem Village forever.

This was only one of the troubles that beset the village. For over a year it had been turned upside down by the witch hunt. Farmers and their wives had dropped everything to attend the examinations. The daily life of others had been disrupted when members of their families were jailed. Fields, gardens and livestock had been neglected. On many a farm in and around Salem Village, there was want.

But worst of all was the guilt. The stain of it could no more be rubbed out by the departure of Mr. Parris than could Lady Macbeth wipe away the blood of the husband she had murdered. Her wail in Shakespeare's tragedy: "All the perfumes of Arabia will not sweeten this little hand," was true of many a hand in Salem Village.

What happened when the witchcraft delusion ended? How did it affect the afflicted girls? Did their torments instantly cease? How did they feel about the sudden collapse of the power and notoriety they had enjoyed?

How did the rest of the people treat them? Was there
any attempt to punish them?

For the most part, there is no answer to these questions. The histories of the village make no mention of
the subject. Historians of the witchcraft delusion say
nothing of it, save for what is known of the afflicted
girls' later lives. Perhaps this is the strongest proof of
the shame that Salem Village felt.

It wanted to forget, but it could not. For years it
was torn by dissension. Families of those who had suffered did not speak to those of the accusers. People
could not meet each other's gaze lest they see there a
reflection of their own shame. Some moved away,
among them Samuel and Mary Sibley (she had given
Tituba the recipe for the "witch cake").

Public sentiment was now overwhelmingly against
the whole witchcraft affair. There were demands that
the colony's government take action to show the people's repentance. The General Court set aside January
15, 1697, as a day of atonement and fasting.

Guilt hung heavy upon many of those who had accused innocent persons or had had a part in sending
them to be executed. No one knows how many repented, for undoubtedly some never confessed it.

Some did, however, though in most cases years passed
before they spoke out. One of the first to do so was
Samuel Sewall, though it took a tragedy in his own
household to bring him to it.

Ever since he had sat on the Court of Oyer and Terminer, Judge Sewall's conscience had plagued him. He

had helped to send nineteen persons to the gallows and Giles Cory to his frightful death. On December 23, 1696, his two-year-old daughter Sarah died. That next night, Christmas Eve, he sat sorrowing in his house on Beacon Hill in Boston.

He handed his Bible to his son Samuel. "Read to me, Sam," he said. "Mayhap I shall find consolation in the Word of God."

His son opened the book to the Gospel according to St. Matthew. The younger Samuel stumbled over the verses, for his father's Bible was in Latin.

Suddenly the judge stiffened and grew tense at the words, "But if ye had known what this meaneth: 'I will have mercy and not sacrifice,' ye would not have condemned the guiltless."

Ye would not have condemned the guiltless. The words struck the judge with terrible force. In his diary for that day he wrote, "Sam. recites to me in Latin Matthew 12 from the 6th to the 12th verses. The 7th verse did awfully bring to mind the Salem Tragedie." Perhaps he wondered whether the vengeful God of the Puritans had taken his child because he too had condemned the guiltless.

A few days later he went to his pastor, the same Samuel Willard who had worked to obtain fair trials for the accused witches.

"I can bear my guilt no longer," he told the minister. "I must make public confession of the wrong I have done by putting up a bill in the church. Will you read it to the congregation on the fast day?"

"Putting up a bill" was a common practice in colonial New England. It was an announcement posted in the church telling of some occasion of joy or sadness which had befallen a man, his family or his intimate friends.

On the fast day the General Court had proclaimed, Samuel Sewall stood humbly before the congregation of the Third Church while Mr. Willard read his confession. From then until the end of his long life, on the anniversary of the fast day, Judge Sewall did penance, the true and sincere repentance of a good man. Save for Nathaniel Saltonstall, who discovered his mistake so early, none of the other judges ever admitted they had been wrong.

In spite of his confession, guilt weighed upon Samuel Sewall's mind for years. As late as 1720 he read a passage in a history of New England about the witchcraft delusion, in which his name was mentioned among the judges. Referring to it, he wrote in his diary, "The good and gracious God be pleased to save New England and me and my family!"

Another confession was made on the fast day. It was a statement signed by Thomas Fisk, the foreman, and the other eleven members of the jury which had reversed its decision and convicted Rebecca Nurse.

"We fear we have been instrumental, with others, though ignorantly and unwittingly, to bring upon ourselves and this people of the Lord the guilt of innocent blood," it said. "We do heartily ask forgiveness of all whom we have offended."

Another man whose conscience would not let him alone was the Beverly minister, John Hale. He had shown Bridget Bishop no mercy when she was accused of killing the insane woman, Christina Trask, by witchcraft. When Goodwife Trask died, Mr. Hale had said she committed suicide. Yet before the Court of Oyer and Terminer he testified the woman had been murdered by supernatural means.

It was a different matter, however, when his own wife was cried out on. She was never arrested, but it made Mr. Hale do some serious thinking. Too many people were being accused. His wife was no witch. There must be others like her . . .

He was still not fully convinced, however. Then came Governor Phips' release of the accused persons who were in prison. Mr. Hale believed the loosing of such a great flock of witches would be a catastrophe. They would surely take revenge, tormenting scores of their accusers. Nothing of the sort happened.

Five years after the end of the witchcraft delusion, Mr. Hale could no longer struggle with his conscience. He wrote a pamphlet called *A Modest Inquiry into the Nature of Witchcraft,* which was published in 1698. In it he admitted he had made mistakes. He said there had been "a going too far in this affair." He added, "It cannot be imagined that in a place of such knowledge, so many in so small a compass of land, should so abominably leap into the Devil's lap at once."

Even Cotton Mather retreated. His sleep at night was disturbed by the fears of a guilty conscience. On November 15, 1696 he wrote in his diary, "Being afflicted last Night with discouraging Thoughts as if . . . the Divine Displeasure must overtake my Family for my not appearing with Vigor enough to stop the proceedings of the Judges when the Inextricable Storm from the Invisible World assaulted the Countrey, I did this morning, in prayer with my Family, putt my Family into the Merciful Hands of the Lord." He added that he had received assurance from the Lord that no vengeance would be taken against him or his family.

One more confession was yet to come. It was by one of the afflicted girls who had done the most, by her accusations and testimony, to send innocent people to Gallows Hill.

Ann Putnam's life, after the witchcraft delusion ended, was not an easy one. Her mother was sick of body as well as mind, and her health declined rapidly. In 1699, when Ann was nineteen, both her parents died within about two weeks of each other. There were younger children in the family, whose care fell upon Ann. The work was hard, she had never been strong, and her health too became poor.

She must have suffered intensely from the guilty knowledge of what she had done. At last, deeply troubled, she went to the Reverend Joseph Green, who had succeeded Mr. Parris as the minister in Salem Village.

"I do not know why I did those grievous things," she told him, "but I must confess my sin before all the people."

"You were very young then," Mr. Green said gently, "and you had fallen under Satan's power. But you are right in wishing to make confession that you were wrong. It will ease the burden upon your soul."

"Will you help me?" Ann pleaded. "I want to beg

forgiveness of all I have wronged, especially Goodwife Nurse's family."

"We will draw up your confession and then discuss it with her son Samuel," said the minister.

There had been great bitterness between the Nurse family and Ann's. It would never be completely forgotten, but Samuel Nurse, after he had read the confession, agreed that it was suitable.

Not only the congregation of the Salem Village meetinghouse, but people from miles around filled every inch of space there on August 25, 1706. The silence when Mr. Green took his place in the pulpit was awesome. There must have been many who contrasted it with the riotous scenes which had taken place there during the examinations of accused witches in 1692.

No one breathed as Ann Putnam rose in her place on the women's side of the broad aisle. She stood with her head bowed.

Mr. Green began to read: "I desire to be humbled before God . . . that I, then being in my childhood, should . . . be made an instrument for the accusation of several persons of a grievous crime, whereby their lives were taken away from them. . . . I now have just grounds and good reason to believe they were innocent persons."

Ann's confession went on to say that what she had done was not due to anger, malice or ill will toward any persons. She said she had done so ignorantly, being deluded by Satan.

Then she concluded: "And particularly since I was a chief instrument of accusing Goodwife Nurse and her two sisters, I desire to lie in the dust and earnestly beg forgiveness of God and from all those unto whom I have given just cause of sorrow and offense, whose relations were taken away and accused."

As far as is known, Ann Putnam was the only one of the afflicted girls who confessed she was wrong or ever showed the slightest remorse for the grief and suffering she had caused.

The First Church in Salem Town also sought to make amends to Rebecca Nurse, who had been so cruelly excommunicated there before her execution. Twenty years later, on March 2, 1712, Rebecca's excommunication was revoked.

So was that of Giles Cory, who had been given the same treatment before he was pressed to death. But in Giles's case the church was not content simply to make atonement for the wrong which had been done him. The document which erased his excommunication stated this was done because he had bitterly repented his refusal to plead either guilty or innocent before the Court of Oyer and Terminer. There is no other record to show that the brave old man retreated an inch from his decision never to be tried for what he had not done.

Could anything else be done to compensate those who had either suffered themselves or had lost relatives? Many of those who had escaped the gallows, and the families of the ones who had not, were determined to have redress from the colony's government.

Philip English was their leader. His anger was hot, perhaps reasonably enough. He had not only lost a large sum in property which had been seized, but his wife

Mary had died soon after they returned to Salem Town from their refuge in New York. Some accounts have it that her death was due to a lung ailment she contracted in the dampness and chill of Boston Prison.

English's rage was directed chiefly at Sheriff George Corwin, who had seized his property. He brought a suit for damages against Corwin in 1694, but the court decided that since the sheriff had only been carrying out official orders he was blameless.

English, still seething, bided his time. His chance for revenge came in 1697, when Corwin died. English rode to the sheriff's house, seized his body, galloped off and hid it. Then he demanded that the family pay him £60 and three shillings. There was a terrible scandal in Salem Town, but before he gave up Corwin's body so that it could be buried, English collected the money.

His hatred also fell upon the Reverend Nicholas Noyes of the First Church in Salem Town. Noyes never admitted that the witch hunts had been wrong, but Philip English publicly called him the murderer of Rebecca Nurse and John Procter. Not only did English never again set foot in Noyes' church, but he founded a new one, St. Peter's, in Salem Town.

He was bitter against John Hathorne too. This feud continued to the end of English's life. Then, as he lay on his deathbed, one of his family suggested that he might like to forgive his one-time friend before he died.

"All right," English growled, "but if I get well I'll be damned if I forgive him!"

In 1709 a group of twenty-one accused witches and the children of those who had died submitted a demand to the General Court that compensation be paid for their sufferings and their good names be completely cleared. Others followed their lead.

Most of the convicted witches had been sent quickly enough to the gallows, but when it came to paying for the damage that had been done, the wheels of justice turned slowly. At last, in 1711, the legislature appropriated £598 and twelve shillings and cleared the accused ones of guilt. Samuel Sewall was appointed head of a committee to distribute the money.

Although this amount would have to be multiplied at least twenty times to make it comparable to money values now, it was a pittance to divide among so many. Philip English alone had demanded £1500 for the devastation the sheriff had wrought upon his property.

Elizabeth Procter, who had been saved from death by Governor Phips' proclamation before her baby was born, received £150 to pay for the loss of her husband and her own sufferings. The large family of the "little black minister" of Casco Bay, George Burroughs, got £50. Sarah Good's brood of children, including poor little Dorcas, whose mind was affected by her ordeal in prison, were given £30.

Others got small amounts too, but Philip English received nothing. Probably, in his anger, he offended some of the committee. The Massachusetts Bay legislature finally agreed to pay £200 for all he had undergone, but by that time he was dead, leaving only his heirs to enjoy the money.

The witchcraft delusion will always be an outstanding event in American history, yet with the passing of many years, people did forget just how terrible it was. The memory was brought back to them with stunning force in the 1950s, however.

Arthur Miller, the eminent playwright, saw that what had happened in 1692 had tremendous dramatic possibilities. His play about it, *The Crucible*, was produced in 1953 and had a long run. It is still often presented in theatres throughout the country.

Audiences gasped at the sufferings of the accused persons, Tituba's black arts and the shocking behavior of the afflicted girls. Also at about this time, a television broadcast dramatized the trial of Ann Pudeator, who was hanged as a witch in Salem Town.

Perhaps *The Crucible* and the television production influenced the Massachusetts legislature to clear the good names of the accused persons and their descendants. On August 28, 1957, it passed a resolution stating that because of the Court of Oyer and Terminer's actions in 1692 "no disgrace attaches to the said descendants or any of them [the accused witches] by reason of such proceedings." The legislators were careful to protect themselves, however, against the possibility that descendants of the accused persons might sue for damages. The resolution stated that it did not include any right to take legal action against the state.

What happened to the chief actors in the tragedy of Salem Village after it ended? Most of them simply disappear from the historical records. Something is known of a few, however.

The Reverend Samuel Parris's later career reminds one of *A Christmas Carol*, by Charles Dickens. It will be remembered that in this famous story the ghosts of persons who had persecuted and cheated others during their lifetimes were doomed to wander the earth forever, trying vainly to help the poor and needy. Mr. Parris wandered too, but his rovings came to an end before his death.

After he was ousted from Salem Village, the minister went to a church in Newton, another of the villages surrounding Boston. From there he moved to Concord. Next, late in 1697, he began preaching at Stow. Since he was the minister in these three places during a period of only about two years, it suggests that either he was unhappy or his congregations were unhappy with him.

Later, Mr. Parris was the pastor of two other churches, first at Dunstable and finally at Sudbury, where he died in 1720. His wife had died at about the time he left Salem Village.

Little Betty Parris went with her father, of course, and so, probably, did Abigail Williams, since she had been adopted by the Parrises. The only other record of the family is that Betty married Benjamin Barnes of Concord in 1710, when she was about twenty-seven years old.

Almost nothing is known of Ann Putnam after her confession in 1706. But her health must have continued to be poor, for she died some ten years later at the age of about thirty-six.

What befell the other afflicted girls remains largely a mystery. It is said that two or three came to bad ends, while Elizabeth Booth and Mary Walcott married and presumably settled down. But how many remained in

Salem Village and how they were treated by other villagers remains a blank. Again, the historians of the village seem to have been reluctant to write of the witchcraft delusion.

Only one man who did write about it tells what happened to Tituba. She was sent to prison in Boston, it will be recalled, after she had confessed to having dealings with Satan. But she was never tried. The only record of her later history is in the writings of Robert Calef, who was a man of mystery himself.

He says that Tituba, being penniless, could not meet the charges which had to be paid before she could be released. Calef claims she remained in prison for some time, and at last, being a slave, she was sold to a new owner for the amount that was due. Of this strange woman's later history and that of her husband John Indian, there is nothing.

More is known of William Stoughton, the merciless chief justice of the Court of Oyer and Terminer and the Superior Court of Adjudicature. His later life brought him one reward which some might say was greater than he deserved.

It happened because hot-tempered Sir William Phips found himself in trouble with his enemies in Massachusetts Bay. Two of them sent a petition to William and Mary, asking that Phips be removed as governor. He straightaway sailed for England to defend himself against the charges. While waiting for his trial to begin, he fell ill and died in 1695.

With that, Stoughton automatically became acting governor. He remained in this post with all the privileges and power of a regular governor until 1699, when a new royal governor was appointed.

There were those who thought there was something strange in the way the Reverend Nicholas Noyes of the First Church in Salem Town died some years after the delusion ended. It has already been told that just before Sarah Good was hanged on Gallows Hill, he shouted that she knew very well she was a witch. Sarah denied it, and then said, "If you take my life, God will give you blood to drink."

Mr. Noyes was a very fat man. Like some other persons who are greatly overweight, he seems to have suffered from high blood pressure, for he died of a burst blood vessel which caused him to bleed internally. Some saw in it the fulfillment of Sarah Good's curse.

These are the scanty details of what is known of the later years of the principal characters in the tragedy of 1692–93. There remains only one big question: Why? What really caused the witchcraft delusion to begin, why did it continue and spread, and why did it end so abruptly and so completely that never again was a "witch" executed in America?

15
Why Did It Happen?

The causes of the witchcraft delusion of 1692–93 in Massachusetts Bay are one of the great mysteries of American history. The puzzle may never be fully solved, for there are conflicting opinions about it.

One widely accepted theory is that of "mass hysteria." It offers a logical explanation for the queer behavior of the girls in Salem Village, though it does not answer all the questions about what happened. Nor do other less accredited theories, such as those based on hypnotism and the beliefs of spiritualism.

Hysteria is a nervous affliction in which people lose control of their emotions. They lose their will power, often suffer imaginary pain and illness, and may go into convulsions or become unconscious. Mass hysteria occurs when a large number of persons become afflicted through contact with others afflicted with hysteria. It is like an epidemic of a disease in which one infected person carries and spreads its germs and infects others, who in turn give the disease to still others.

Sigmund Freud, the father of modern psychiatry, wrote about hysteria. He said it could be caused by an attempt to "push away" something.

This could have happened to little Betty Parris, the first of the girls in Salem Village to become afflicted. Since she was only nine, whatever she learned from Tituba probably made a very strong impression on her young mind. And since she was the daughter of a Puritan minister, she would have had guilty feelings over the things Tituba told her and Abigail Williams.

The Puritan religion was one of repression—"thou shalt not." Over and over, its ministers told their congregations what they must avoid because it was sinful. A great many things were. It was not only wrong to do them, but even to think of doing them. So when Tituba imparted some of her evil knowledge of obeah and the "black art" to impressionable Betty Parris and Abigail Williams, Betty's mind would instinctively have tried to "push away" what she had learned because it was sinful.

Abigail Williams was two years older, but still very young. She too would have been impressed and a little fearful of what she had learned from Tituba. Since she lived in the same house with Betty, it was quite natural that she would be the first to become infected with her cousin's hysteria.

Although the Parrises tried to keep what had happened a secret, it soon leaked out. The other girls who had attended the sessions with Tituba and who were older, then "caught" the hysteria. First it was Mary Walcott and Susanna Sheldon, probably because they lived nearest to the parsonage and saw Betty and Abigail oftener. Then Ann Putnam fell a victim to the mysterious ailment.

Ann was a likely victim of mass hysteria. She was a nervous little girl. Moreover, her mother was even more high-strung.

Mr. Bayley, the minister who had married Goodwife Putnam's sister, had been hounded by his congregation until he left Salem Village. Goodwife Bayley, the Bayley children and some of Goodwife Putnam's own children had died. Ann's mother suspected these deaths were not natural, and she wanted to know the truth of it. When she heard that Tituba could get in touch with the spirits of the dead, she sent her daughter to find out.

Of course, Ann did not doubt her mother's beliefs. Whatever she learned from Tituba that day at the parsonage, as well as later on, must have had a tremendous impact on her, just as it did on Betty Parris and Abigail Williams.

Then it began to be whispered about the village that something was wrong with Betty and Abigail. One can imagine the scene when Goodwife Putnam finally learned just what it was. Ann would have listened, wide-eyed, as her parents discussed it. Goodwife Putnam's querulous voice and the fanatical light in her eyes must have been enough to send a terrified shudder through Ann as she heard the details, some true, some doubtless enlarged by her mother's sharp imagination.

Goodwife Putnam would have had her suspicions: "Don't tell *me* it's just distemper! It's some mischief of Satan's that's afoot! Mark you, there's those in this village know more'n they're telling about it . . . !"

If Ann sensed what her mother was driving at, the thought would have darted into her mind: *bewitched?* Was that what was wrong with Betty and Abigail? But she herself had been often at the parsonage with them and Tituba . . .

All this may have caused the strange affliction to seize Ann Putnam. By hearing, by seeing, by imagining—in such ways mass hysteria spreads.

Were the girls actually tormented? Did they really see, feel and hear someone or something biting, pinching and threatening them? Did they see the bizarre shapes of those they accused, see the birds, dogs, hogs and other witches' "familiars" through which the devil was supposed to work his evil designs?

Probably all of them did, at least some of the time. Freud wrote that it is quite possible for some hysterical persons to see strange things, feel very real pain and go into fits in which they become paralyzed.

Many people, of course, said afterwards that the girls were shamming, that they "put on an act" and were not really tormented. But if their agonies were not real, then an extraordinary number of gifted actresses lived in Salem Village. No play can succeed unless the members of the cast make the audience believe it. Few people have such talent, and it takes hard work and long practice to develop it. The girls had no such preparation, yet they made their audiences believe, including the ministers, judges and magistrates.

The evidence is strong that they did suffer. It was not always their agony that made them cry out on people, however. Some of the girls, especially the older ones, were spiteful. At times, when their affliction left them and they became quite normal, they were vengeful.

One such instance was caused by John Procter, who had threatened his servant girl, Mary Warren, with a whipping. He spoke his mind in public one day about all the girls.

"They should all be at the whipping post!" he stormed. "If they are let alone we will all be devils and witches!" His rage boiled over and he raised his voice to a shout: "Hang them! Hang them!"

The story was all over the village in no time, and of course the girls heard it. As has been seen, their spite was first directed against John Procter's wife.

One of the girls, whose name the records do not mention, was in Ingersoll's tavern one day when she went into a fit and shrieked, "There's Goody Procter! Old witch, I'll have her hang!"

To her astonishment, the startled patrons in the tavern refused to believe she had seen Goodwife Procter's "shape." They looked in the direction she was pointing and said they couldn't see anything. One spoke up: "You are lying."

The girl came out of her trance. "It was for sport," she mumbled. "I must have some sport." Whether her fit was real or not, it had now left her, but she was still vindictive.

No one knows why Mary Warren decided that those she had accused were innocent. But it is hard to believe that the way some of the girls turned on her was anything but vengeful.

Reputable medical observers of hysteria say that its victims sometimes use it to punish someone they do not like. Such persons may even deliberately prolong their hysteria in order to spite an enemy. Thus the afflicted girls could have used it intentionally to gain revenge over those who tried to thwart them—the Procters, Mary Warren and others.

Although mass hysteria seems a logical explanation for the outbreak of the witchcraft delusion, other powerful influences helped to keep it going. One was the notoriety which came to the girls.

Life in Salem Village was very dull. Even such innocent amusements as the huskings which were sometimes held were frowned upon by the austere Puritan ministers. There was not a theatre in all Massachusetts Bay. Christmas was not celebrated; it was considered a pagan holiday. Dancing and playing cards were the devil's own devices.

As for the girls themselves, they were of no importance in Salem Village. The servant girls' conduct was strictly regulated by their masters. So was that of the younger ones by their parents. The old adage that children should be seen and not heard was never more true than in the Puritan families of the village.

Then, suddenly, the afflicted girls were famous. Not only neighbors but people from all the surrounding villages flocked in to watch their strange antics. The examinations and trials were crowded with pop-eyed spectators.

If the girls were a little dazed at first, they soon saw how pleasant and flattering it all was. Life became exciting indeed. Naturally they did not want to give it up and go back to the old humdrum existence.

For the first time too, they knew what it was like to have power. Scarcely anyone questioned the girls' charges; few of those who did doubt them dared speak out. Ministers came, staring open-mouthed and shaking their heads in awe. Such eminent and learned men as the Mathers believed. Magistrates and judges accepted the girls' testimony without objection. And the power these children and maidservants wielded was terrible, for they could put anyone they wished under the shadow of the gallows. So they became arrogant, feeling themselves little empresses.

They had their moments of fear, however, for once they had begun they dared not stop. Mary Warren tried and found herself accused and in prison. If the rest had allowed Mary to back down, the whole witchcraft affair might have collapsed. Then the whole colony would have turned against them.

The hardest thing to understand is why the learned men of Massachusetts Bay believed. But the world of the seventeenth century was vastly different from that of three centuries later. And for hundreds of years people had believed in witches.

The Book of Exodus in the Old Testament contains laws to be obeyed by the people. They include the one which says, "Thou shalt not suffer a witch to live."

In biblical days there appear to have been persons who claimed to be witches or sorcerers. Thus it is not strange to find injunctions in the Bible against those who offended God by claiming to have godlike powers themselves.

What happened in Salem Village was quite different. No one who was accused had claimed to be a witch. No one voluntarily confessed to being one. Except perhaps for one or two whose minds were affected, those who confessed when they were questioned did so only in the hope of saving themselves.

Nevertheless, it was the law of the Old Testament that a witch must not live. Massachusetts Bay was settled as a Puritan theocracy; that is, its laws were based upon those in the Bible rather than on the Common Law of England, which had developed over centuries of experience. As time went on, more and more of the principles of Common Law came into use, but in 1692 Massachusetts Bay was still basically a theocracy.

It must be remembered that most of the Massachusetts Bay ministers were fanatical men where the laws of the Bible were concerned. They believed in the strictest interpretation of those laws. And they sincerely believed that Satan was at work in the colony through witches who had sold their souls to him. Under the biblical law they must be found and destroyed. The ministers set the example for everyone else, for they were the most learned men of the colony.

Another thing about the witchcraft delusion which is difficult to understand concerns its ending. It would probably have come to an end gradually anyhow in 1693, for it had gone too far. More and more persons were being jailed when jealous or malicious neighbors accused them. People were beginning to see how ridiculous it was. And there was fear in everyone's heart. No one was safe.

But it did not die slowly. Once Sir William Phips acted, it collapsed like a building dynamited into rubble. And with its end, the afflicted girls' mouths were stopped just as abruptly. If they were truly afflicted, how could their torments have ended so suddenly?

Perhaps the ability of those suffering from hysteria to prolong it in order to gain revenge also gives a clue to the sudden ending of the girls' affliction. They may have had enough control over it to stop as well as prolong it. Certainly, action by the governor of the colony must have frightened them.

Some good did come out of the witchcraft delusion, even though it was gained at such a terrible price. People throughout the American colonies were horrified and revolted once they realized what a frightful injustice had been done. Execution for witchcraft was ended forever in America. In that way, at least, it had beneficial results.

The delusion also had a strong influence toward ending such witch hunts in Britain as well. England and Scotland were slower than America in doing so, but in England executions were ended after a woman and her nine-year-old daughter were hanged for witchcraft in 1716. The last one took place in Scotland in 1722. And in 1736 King George II abolished prosecution for witchcraft in both countries.

The blame for the witchcraft delusion of 1692–93 does not rest upon ministers, judges, the accusers or anyone else. It was caused by ignorance. Not only the mass of the common people, but those who were considered learned were ignorant of the truth that there was no such thing as a witch.

Even in our much more civilized world today, belief in witchcraft and other forms of the "black art" still persists. In some of the West Indian islands obeah is still practiced in spite of strict laws against it. Some tribes in the remote parts of Africa have their witch doctors. Even in the mountainous "backwoods" sections of the United States there are people who believe in witches and "hants." But as wider education throughout the world banishes ignorance, these beliefs too will die out.

The Greek philosopher Diogenes Laertius, speaking of Socrates, wrote, "He said there was only one good, namely, knowledge; and only one evil, ignorance."

Ignorance was the evil in Massachusetts Bay in 1692; knowledge would have saved it from the greatest shame in its history.

16

And Today

Most people think of Salem, Massachusetts (Salem Town, it was then), as where it all happened. Thousands of people go there each year to visit the "Witch House," once the home of the magistrate, Jonathan Corwin, and the place where the jury went from the courthouse to decide the fate of poor Rebecca Nurse. Tourists also go to the "Old Witch Jail," probably containing some of the timbers of the one demolished in 1813, in which accused witches were imprisoned in 1692–93. Some visit Gallows Hill to see where the nineteen convicted witches were executed. And the visitors buy souvenirs—witch dolls riding broomsticks and the like. Salem is famous as the town of the witches.

True, much of the drama which has made the witchcraft delusion famous took place in Salem. But it began in Danvers, then Salem Village. There lived the people who played most of the leading roles—the afflicted girls, Tituba, Mr. Parris, Rebecca Nurse, Giles and Martha Cory, Sarah Osburne and other unforgettable characters. There most of the examinations of accused witches were held. Yet in comparison to Salem, Danvers is less known to the public.

There is little about Danvers today to suggest that once, considering its size, it was as dreadful a place as was Paris a century later during the French Revolution, when hundreds of people went to the guillotine in the Reign of Terror. It looks much like many other towns that cluster around the rim of Boston. It has many attractive, well-kept houses and a flourishing business section.

Two houses where accused witches lived still stand—the Rebecca Nurse house and the Osburne house. In the latter a descendant of Sarah Osburne lives. Danvers is content to point them out with inconspicuous historical markers. No signs advertise: "See where the witches lived!" or "Danvers, the Witch Town." Modern "witch hunters" are well repaid, however, by searching out these places.

The Nurse house is set well back from Pine Street on a narrow lane. Nothing is easier to believe than that a witch once lived in this "salt box" house, with its tremendously long, sloping roof on one side and short, steep-pitched one on the other, and its two great chimneys. There is something gloomy and foreboding about it.

The house was built more than three centuries ago, in 1636, and it may well stand for many more years, for it has been lovingly preserved by the Rebecca Nurse Association, a group of descendants and others, who bought it in 1907.

It is easy to imagine a witch living in the Osburne house too. It stands on Maple Street, on the outskirts of town, having been moved there from its original site some distance farther out. A big, stout dwelling, it is weatherbeaten and its windows are divided into the small square panes which in colonial times were known as quarrels. Parts of it have been rebuilt because of fires which have occurred there, but much of it is just as it was when "Witch Osburne" lived there.

What originally was the village center of Salem Village is not in the middle of Danvers, but also on the outskirts. The old meetinghouse where the examinations of so many accused witches were held is long gone, but its lineal descendant stands in its place. Deacon Ingersoll's tavern was just across the road, and a short distance beyond is the site of Mr. Parris's parsonage and the famous pasture where the afflicted girls saw the "witches' Sabbath" being held. But without knowing where to look, people would pass the old village center by, unnoticed.

Salem Village wanted nothing so much as to forget when the witchcraft delusion was over. In 1752 it changed its name. Histories of the town are vague about why it was renamed Danvers. One explanation given is that Spencer Phips, nephew and adopted son of Sir William, who was then acting governor of Massachusetts Bay, was a close friend of a British nobleman, Sir Danvers Osburne, one of the colonial governors of New York. There is no indication that he was in any way related to the Osburnes who were involved in the witchcraft troubles.

And why did the village change its name? One answer seems to be that it wanted to be separate from Salem proper, of which it was really a part. But one wonders whether the people of Salem Village felt that a new name would help them forget . . .

For a long time Danvers made little effort to attract visitors to the scenes of the witchcraft delusion. It was almost as if, even after more than two and a half centuries, it still preferred not to be reminded of the past and to remain little known.

Yet it was known to many young people who studied American history and learned about that terrible year of 1692. A flood of requests each year from students asking about the landmarks of what was once Salem Village impelled the Danvers Chamber of Commerce to provide more information about them. With the cooperation of the Historic Commission of Danvers, it issued and distributes leaflets describing these landmarks and a map showing how visitors can reach them.

It is well that they can. In 1692 the victims of the witch hunt found no justice to enable them to prove their innocence. The landmarks which are left today stand as reminders to all liberty-loving people that justice under the law must be preserved as one of the precious freedoms upon which our nation was founded in 1776.

SUGGESTIONS FOR FURTHER READING

Out of over 60 sources consulted in the writing of this book, it is not easy to assemble a list of titles suggested for further reading on the subject of witchcraft and the witchcraft delusion in Massachusetts Bay in 1692–93. The majority of the books were published long ago and are unlikely to be found in modern school libraries or, indeed, anywhere but in the reference collections of libraries in the largest cities.

Probably the best modern work on the witchcraft delusion in Massachusetts Bay is *The Devil in Massachusetts*, by Marion L. Starkey (New York: Knopf, 1949). It is accurate, comprehensive and easy to read, and it contains much information on the examinations and trials of the accused witches which had to be omitted in this book.

Here are some other important sources consulted:

Freud, Sigmund. *Selected Papers on Hysteria and Other Psychological Neuroses.* New York: Nervous and Mental Diseases Publishing Co., 1920.
Kittredge, George Lyman. *Witchcraft in Old and New England.* Cambridge: Harvard University Press, 1928.

Levin, David. *What Happened in Salem?* New York: Harcourt, Brace & World, 1960.

Lounsberry, Alice. *Sir William Phips.* New York: Scribner, 1941.

Maple, Eric. *The Dark World of Witches.* London: Robert Hale, Ltd., 1962.

Perley, M. V. B. *A Short History of the Salem Witchcraft Trials.* Salem: M. V. B. Perley, Publisher, 1911.

Sergeant, Philip W. *Witches and Warlocks.* London: Hutchinson & Co., 1936.

Upham, Charles W. *Salem Witchcraft.* New York: Frederick Ungar Publishing Co., 1959.

Index

Index

About the Author

CLIFFORD LINDSEY ALDERMAN was born in Springfield, Massachusetts, educated in public schools there and at the U.S. Naval Academy. He has traveled all over the world, both as a tourist and in connection with his writing, since he likes to know at first hand the places he writes about. He is the author of a number of books, for both adults and young people.